ADHD AND EMOTIONAL INTELLIGENCE

POSITIVE PARENTING TECHNIQUES TO USE WHEN RAISING AN EXPLOSIVE CHILD WITH ATTENTION DEFICIT HYPERACTIVITY DISORDER

ROXANA C.

© **Copyright 2022 - All rights reserved.**

The content contained within this book may not be reproduced, duplicated or transmitted without direct written permission from the author or the publisher.

Under no circumstances will any blame or legal responsibility be held against the publisher, or author, for any damages, reparation, or monetary loss due to the information contained within this book, either directly or indirectly.

Legal Notice:

This book is copyright protected. It is only for personal use. You cannot amend, distribute, sell, use, quote or paraphrase any part, or the content within this book, without the consent of the author or publisher.

Disclaimer Notice:

Please note the information contained within this document is for educational and entertainment purposes only. All effort has been executed to present accurate, up to date, reliable, complete information. No warranties of any kind are declared or implied. Readers acknowledge that the author is not engaged in the rendering of legal, financial, medical or professional advice. The content within this book has been derived from various sources. Please consult a licensed professional before attempting any techniques outlined in this book.

By reading this document, the reader agrees that under no circumstances is the author responsible for any losses, direct or indirect, that are incurred as a result of the use of the information contained within this document, including, but not limited to, errors, omissions, or inaccuracies.

CONTENTS

Introduction   7

1. WHAT IS GOING ON WITH MY KID?   19
   - Children With ADHD   22
   - Exploring the Symptoms   23
   - Inattentiveness   25
   - Hyperactivity   31
   - Impulsivity   34
   - Boys, Girls, and ADHD   36
   - ADHD, Among Other Things   43
   - Are They Naughty, Or Is It ADHD?   51
   - Positive Parenting Tip   57

2. MOMMY, DADDY, CAN YOU SEE ME?   61
   - Case Studies   62
   - ADHD, With Emphasis on Disorder   70

3. THE NEUROSCIENCE OF ADHD   81
   - Causes of ADHD   82
   - The ADHD Brain Versus a Neurotypical Brain   86

4. DIAGNOSING ADHD AND TREATMENT OPTIONS   93
   - Should I Get My Child Diagnosed?   94
   - Getting a Proper Diagnosis   97
   - Types of Positive Diagnosis   100
   - ADHD Treatment Options   102
   - Positive Parenting Tip   111

5. STRENGTHEN THE BODY AND CALM
   THE BRAIN   115
   Cultivating a Healthy and Balanced
   Lifestyle for Your Child   116

6. MANAGING EMOTIONS   137
   Becoming Emotionally Intelligent   138
   ADHD and the Brain Connections   141
   The Steps to Becoming More
   Emotionally Intelligent   143
   Helping Your Child Identify and Express
   Emotions   147
   The Best Way to Teach is by Modeling
   Desired Behavior   155
   Identify What Caused the Feelings   156
   Focusing on Anger   156
   Ask for Help   159

7. HEALING THE PAST AND THE
   FUTURE   161
   A 360-Degree Approach   163
   Techniques to Help Equip Your Child for
   Trauma Recovery   167
   ADHD, Trauma, and Self-Esteem   169

8. ADHD, SOCIALLY SPEAKING   177
   The Social Struggles Your Child Is Facing   178
   Social Anxiety and ADHD   181
   Helping Your Child Overcome Social
   Anxiety   182

9. THE ADHD TEEN   193
   Challenging Social Situations   195
   How to Help Your Child Navigate Life
   Through Teenage Years   199
   Handling Emotional Dysregulation   203
   Tips for Teens   205

10. EVERYDAY COPING TOOLS 209
   Focus 209
   Transitions 211
   ADHD Rush 213
   Meals 215
   Losing Things 216
   Accidents 218
   Homework Battles 219
   Choosing the Right School 220
   Teachers 221

Conclusion 223
References 229

INTRODUCTION

I thought a lot about how to begin this book, as it deals with a sensitive subject, a fascinating subject, and a controversial subject: attention deficit hyperactivity disorder, better known as ADHD.

I, personally, have a great sensitivity to this subject, and you will understand this along the way, so I've decided to start this book by thanking you: Thank you for caring. If you look for a book, material, or anything about this subject, it means that you care about it, and for that, you have my respect.

Between taking things for granted, asking questions, and looking for solutions, there is a very thin line, but unfortunately, not everyone manages to tread it. For that, you need a special sensitivity—you need to be able to see, and want to see, when someone needs your help. That person might be your child, student, grandchild, or friend, but it is up to you to invest your energy into that caring. It means opening your heart and dedicating the most important thing we humans have to someone else: our time.

In daily life, any task can be done in two ways: It can be done because it must or "has to be" done, or it can be done with love, with passion. When working with a material object or an impersonal thing, the two types of actions can have the same result. Nothing out of place, objective.

However, it is completely different when we work with people. Why? Because people feel. You feel the difference. Your child feels it. Life coach and therapist, Shannon L. Alder, reminds us for this very reason, "Never give up on someone with a mental illness. When "I" is replaced by "We", illness becomes wellness" (n.d.).

Consider the following scenario: You're at the park watching your child swinging upside down by the monkey bars, or running in circles around the swingset while they narrowly dodge the swinger's dangerous kicks, or throwing handfuls of gravel up into the air, laughing with glee as they get hit by the painful shower.

You smile. Your child is having a grand ol' time. Suddenly, a "helpful parent" steps in. They say something like, "You sure do have your hands full." You smile again. Little do they know how full your hands *actually* are.

Though your child is having fun now, an hour before you left for the park, a whirlwind occurred. There was screaming, howling, crying, and rolling on the floor, all because the little guy couldn't find his favorite socks. Could this have been the real reason? We don't know. Where were the socks? On his bookshelf, you *eventually* discovered.

As you got into the car, and all the "drama" had passed, you were happy. Finally, you are going to the park. He will enjoy this. Then, your child cracked a joke that made your stomach hurt from laughing so hard, and all that, right before he let you know that his class has a huge project due the next day. You are hearing about this project for the first time *today*, right now, on your way to the park. Does this sound familiar?

Unfortunately, parents of children with ADHD tend to be painted in a bad light, and that stigma only extends further to our children themselves. They are assumed to be "handfuls," "lazy," or "bratty," without any consideration by others as to the truth of their lived experiences.

Now, in our scenario, you wait quietly on the bench until your child gets bored of playing, so you can go home as soon as possible. During this time, you start planning the rest of the day in your mind, including doing the project for school.

Having a child with ADHD can be challenging. Hell, having a neurotypical child can be challenging. And, as with any other, having a child with ADHD can feel downright nightmarish on some days. It can feel like the only way you could possibly succeed as a parent is by obtaining superpowers, like telepathy: How nice it would be to find out exactly what they mean when they say something *"tastes loud"*?!

While it may not be a superpower, developing unique strategies for daily challenges you and your child face can create a happy and somewhat stress-free environment for you both.

ADHD is known to be "a neurological and behavioral disorder that affects the person with it and the entire family, including parents and the extended family of parental siblings and grandparents. It tests the limits of the family's ability to be supportive, understanding, and loving" (Dahl, 2022). Many well-known parenting hacks won't always work for you because many of those tips are built around neurotypical children. Not every child is neurotypical.

In fact, 9.8% of children—around 6 million in the United States of America—between the ages of three and seventeen were diagnosed with ADHD in the period of 2016-2019 (National Center for Birth Defects and Developmental Disabilities, 2022). Additionally, it's important to remember that not all cases of any condition are diagnosed. This means that over 1 in 10 people are likely to have ADHD. So, perhaps you may not have ADHD, but it is very likely that you know someone who does.

ADHD is real and valid. The sooner we recognize the patterns and learn to work with these kids, the better assured we will be that they, as adults, will be healthy members of society.

— RHONDA VAN DIEST

The sad truth of the matter is that many children with ADHD grow up without ever learning the necessary skills and strategies needed to cope with their disorder. On top of ADHD, they struggle with anxiety, stress, depression, and constant overwhelm. It's a continuous battle in their heads, and they don't know how to cope with or manage these emotions.

Diagnosed children must face the stigmas surrounding ADHD, while the undiagnosed face the challenges of being completely misunderstood. Yet, everyone with ADHD deserves access to proper management techniques that work for their brain.

Much like many other mental health and brain disorders, ADHD is hugely misunderstood, misconstrued, and stigmatized. So much of the condition is swept under the carpet—truly inhibiting diagnosis—while other parts of the disorder are advertised as being "not that serious." Sure, people with ADHD struggle to focus and can get distracted, but you can just do some breathing exercises and still your mind, right? Not quite. You can't exactly think your way out of physiological differences in your brain.

Mental illness is nothing to be ashamed of, but stigma and bias shame us all.

— PRESIDENT BILL CLINTON

It is, of course, only normal for any parent to hope their child's impulsive ADHD-prompted behavior will improve as they grow older. And yes, sometimes, some of the symptoms—like fidgeting, daydreaming, and forgetfulness—can improve as they age. Yet, in most cases, ADHD is not a concern kids just outgrow.

For the longest time, people—including the experts in the field—used to think that when a child reached their teenage years, there was a 50% chance that their symptoms would improve. More recent studies have shown that these assumptions were wrong as, in most cases, this doesn't happen. It can occur that the symptoms improve or change as the child matures, but they don't disappear. Rather, this perceived improvement is often a hard-earned self-taught skill practiced by many adults with ADHD to avoid social ridicule or employment difficulties in a world built for the neurotypical brain.

As a result of this misunderstanding of the condition, approximately 60% of ADHD kids grow up without learning the crucial skills and strategies that they need to survive. While their parents assume that they will "grow out of" disruptive or debilitating behavior, growing children still struggle with the limiting symptoms that come with mismanagement. Many become boomerang kids, repeatedly moving back in with their parents as adults or maybe never leaving. Many more struggle with stress, anxiety, depression, and overwhelm.

There is so much stigma, stereotyping, and misunderstanding about ADHD getting in the way of our ability to deal with it effectively. Stereotypically, kids with ADHD tend to run, squirm, and not focus in class or complete their assignments. They often talk out of turn, cut lines, and act impulsively, and because their behavior isn't socially acceptable, they are often misunderstood or even excluded by their peers. When they grow up, these children become adults who no longer portray their symptoms externally, instead turning their behavior inwards. Now, they are bored, restless, and shame-filled adults.

Despite the ways that ADHD is often misunderstood, over recent years, we've witnessed an increase in diagnoses of ADHD. Thankfully, this rise in numbers is likely due to more children being tested now than before, more accurate testing measures, or other external causes. Yet, while research in this field has taken giant steps of progress, we still have many unanswered questions, and more research is certainly needed to fill the gaps in our knowledge and understanding of ADHD.

We know that the symptoms of this condition can change but seldom go away. Research shows that it runs in families and has a genetic link, but it can't say yet what causes one sibling to have ADHD while another is entirely neurotypical altogether. Later in this book, we will also explore how it is not only genetics that contributes to the presence of ADHD.

However, in my family, it is *definitely* genetic. My mother has ADHD, and I have ADHD, and that certainly came with its challenges—particularly as neither of us were aware of our condition throughout my childhood. I can't say that I was always unhappy throughout those early years, but God, it was hard. As a child, I faced many challenges. I constantly felt like I had to do more to achieve at the same level as my peers. I constantly felt like I was falling behind and would never catch up. I had almost all the symptoms.

Yet, at the time, I didn't understand how obvious that was. Alder (n.d.) describes that I was certainly not alone in this:

> Not enough people realize that ADHD is not a disorder about loss of focus. It is a disorder of loss of emotional control, which is triggered by outside influences, self-esteem, and our interpretation of events. Whether this is positive or negative, it triggers us to hyper-focus on what consumes our thoughts. Staying positive is critical, and distancing oneself from hurtful people is essential in order to live a life with purpose.

I argued with my peers and my parents non-stop. My parents looked permanently disappointed with me. It hurt me the most when I saw they couldn't understand me. Truly, I felt like I might never find peace. Though it came very late, fortunately, I was eventually diagnosed with ADHD, and suddenly, everything clicked.

A significant realization that came along with my diagnosis was in relation to the troubled relationship between my parents and myself. I could suddenly understand all the arguments we had had over time. I realized how different our minds were and how much we struggled to communicate with each other. Even if it sounds cliché, I have to tell you that communication is, and always will be, the key. But first, you have to understand where the problem lies, and I struggled to understand this for years.

It was an enormous mental effort to catch up on these years spent in ignorance of my own neurotype. I didn't limit myself to understanding myself. I tried to understand my parents as well, especially my mother, who had no idea she had ADHD, and my father, who has temperament problems. Our quarrels often ended with the phrase, "It's like a madhouse here." As an adult, I now recognize the lack of understanding and efficient communication.

When you have a peaceful life in childhood, you have hobbies, you are passionate about specific fields, and later on, you might even become a specialist in that matter. Then, you call it a career. Instead, my only concern throughout a large portion of my life was to solve my problems and my family's problems or at least know how to deal with them and, hopefully, one day, to make it alright for once. And so, because this was the drama of my life, I couldn't think of anything more than how to fix myself and my parents. I spent all my time on this matter. My diagnosis filled that gap, and I was able to repair the relationship that had been built on mutual ignorance.

I write this book from the perspective of a fellow human being who struggled with this my entire life. I write this book in the hope that I can offer you insight into your child's unique mind. I hope that this insight will help you establish a strong bond with them through which you can help them navigate the daily struggles they face.

I recognize the reality that many parents are overworked, struggling financially, stressed, overwhelmed, and dealing with their own demands. However, I also acknowledge that too many children are raised through fear and force rather than receiving the education and support they desperately need. Unfortunately, this turns into a vicious cycle where children who are not taught proper ways to cope become overwhelmed and stressed-out adults who, in turn, don't know how to teach their children healthy ways to cope.

By picking up this book, recognize that you want to break this cycle. You are one of the powerful few who have identified this problem and wish to educate and support your child. You are fighting for a change. Many adults, like me, did not get the support we needed because, back then, there was little awareness and zero support for children like us. We just needed to figure it out somehow, and we either sank or swam.

If you are reading this book, this puts you in the small but powerful number of parents fighting for change for their children and all the ADHD children of the world. Let's get started on those vital life skills that will ensure your kids succeed.

1

WHAT IS GOING ON WITH MY KID?

Before a diagnosis—and sometimes even after—you may not know exactly what your child is dealing with and what this means. You probably sometimes find yourself looking at your child and wondering, *Is it normal for them to behave like this?* This is a question that perhaps every parent asks about their child, regardless of their neurotype. We want to do everything right, we want happy children, and again we ask ourselves, "Do I know what I'm doing as a parent?"

Sometimes, the answer to that question is, "No, something must be out of place. The other parents don't seem to find it so difficult. How do they succeed? Ugh, if only it were that easy for me too." I understand you.

How do we distinguish a natural childish behavior from one showing signs of ADHD? The truth is that each and every child on this planet is a unique and individual being. What may be true for one is likely untrue for the next. One child might be particularly fond of sharks, while the next is utterly terrified of them.

Categorizing kids is never an easy or effective task. Not all sporty kids play hockey—some play soccer. Not all arty kids like painting—some will prefer to sculpt. Similarly, not all neurodivergent kids are struggling with the same issues. You might argue that neurodivergent is a medical term, and therefore, it should spell out a definitive list of associated actions and behaviors, attaching certain aspects to a person labeled with the term. But then, we could say the same of the word "neurotypical," and not all kids who are neurotypical are the same, are they? Just as each neurotypical brain has different strengths and weaknesses, so do the brains of those who are neurodivergent.

The one thing that all children have in common is that they all have struggles and challenges.

> Cherish the children marching to the beat of their own music. They play the most beautiful heart songs.
>
> — FIONA GOLDSWORTHY

You may

- already know your child's diagnosis and know what you're facing.
- have a diagnosis you are not 100% sure is accurate for your child.
- not have a diagnosis.
- not even know if your child's behavior warrants a diagnosis at all.

Many different behaviors can indicate many different things. Not to mention that "Behavior isn't something someone has. Rather, it emerges from the interaction of a person's biology, past experiences, and immediate context." (*A Quote by L. Todd Rose*, n.d.).

That said, your child's behavior may indicate one possible explanation but actually mean something else. It can be difficult to determine when a diagnosis is necessary and when the diagnosis given is accurate. It can be helpful, in this regard, to be aware of some of the "typical" symptoms of ADHD so that you know what to look out for.

CHILDREN WITH ADHD

Most positive ADHD diagnoses occur before a child turns 12; though this is not always the case as many people, myself included, only receive a diagnosis much later in life, even in adulthood. As a result of the slant toward childhood diagnoses, parents and teachers can often be the first to recognize when an individual is displaying the symptoms of attention deficit hyperactivity disorder (ADHD). Therefore, it is vital that adults learn to recognize ADHD—sometimes mistakenly called attention deficit disorder (ADD)—for what it truly is and discard myths or outdated beliefs about the condition.

For instance, the wider public often incorrectly uses the above terms, ADHD and ADD, interchangeably, but it is important to note the distinctions between these abbreviations: ADD is the colloquial term for one particular type of ADHD—the predominantly inattentive type (discussed further later in this chapter), formerly called attention deficit disorder:

> "Technically speaking, ADD is no longer a medical diagnosis, but 'ADD' is often used to

refer to predominantly inattentive type ADHD and its associated symptoms. Since 1994, doctors have used the term ADHD to describe both the hyperactive and inattentive subtypes of attention deficit hyperactivity disorder. Still, many parents, teachers, and adults continue to use the term 'ADD.'" (Russo & ADHD Editorial Board, 2022 para 3).

EXPLORING THE SYMPTOMS

When educating ourselves on ADHD, it is vital to learn to recognize the symptoms of this condition. However, this wealth of information can sometimes be cognitively overwhelming when received all at once. To help you determine the implications of these symptoms for your own child, please consider the following points when reading the following section:

- If it looks like your child is exhibiting some of the behavior referenced here, that does not necessarily mean they have ADHD. It merely indicates that it would be helpful to schedule an appointment with a mental healthcare professional to determine what (if any) diagnosis and treatment should be applied.

- If your child is not exhibiting all of the behavior referenced here, that does not mean they don't have ADHD. As you may still be concerned about your child since they are still portraying some of the symptoms, it might still be best to schedule that appointment.
- With or without a diagnosis, your child will still need your love, support, and attention, and they deserve the best parental care.
- Sometimes, even without a diagnosis, your child may need a little extra help to manage their social skills and responsibilities.

Specialists categorize the symptoms of ADHD into two categories: inattentiveness and hyperactivity/impulsiveness

As your child goes through the diagnostic process, it may be discovered that your child presents with symptoms of only one category or both. Quite often, the symptoms of ADHD are most prevalent in children and teenagers, and they can improve as the child ages. Yet, when adults receive a positive diagnosis, it is because they are still challenged by the symptoms of the concern, and therefore, we can't say that children will "outgrow" any diagnosis.

INATTENTIVENESS

Most teachers and adults could benefit from pretending that all kids in their class have ADHD —what is good for kids with ADHD is good for all kids.

— DR. EDWARD M. HALLOWELL

Paying attention in class was one of my biggest challenges. Initially, I thought it was because of the language—as I studied abroad for a while—but no, wherever I was, my thoughts kept on rolling and rolling. This was due to my inability to remain on topic. I remember the teacher often asking me something while I wasn't paying attention, and I was always embarrassed that I needed to ask her to repeat herself. But I made my class laugh—I was "so silly." Later in life, I realized that it was in my own interest to be attentive, and I started to put more effort into it. Yet, even as I tried my hardest, my experience at school became accompanied by a permanent fear and a feeling that I was "left behind." I understand now that it would be challenging for any teacher to have kids in their class who are different from the set mold of conformity. But it wasn't my ability to remain attentive that left me scared but rather the incredible burden of criticism due to a lack of understanding of my condition—including self-blame due to my own failure to grasp my situation.

Today, there is a growing understanding that it's not that a kid dealing with inattentiveness *doesn't want to* pay attention or *chooses* not to focus; ADHD makes it extremely difficult, if not *impossible*, for them to do so. As parents and teachers often misread the child's behavior as unwillingness, children facing this concern can go undiagnosed for quite some time. This is why it is so vital that parents and teachers cooperate to identify symptoms and better understand a child's behavior. Only once a neurodivergent child has been diagnosed can proper measures be put in place to best support the child.

The Symptoms of Inattentiveness

As we explore the symptoms of inattentiveness, keep in mind that for a child to be formally diagnosed with ADHD, they would need to present with at least six of the following symptoms over six months, generally first noticed before they turned 12.

Easily Distracted

It may be expected for any child to get distracted from a task they don't care for or aren't interested in doing, but when a child receives a positive diagnosis of inattentive ADHD, they are often very distractable, even when they are busy with tasks they do enjoy. For instance, the child might get distracted or walk away while mid-conversation.

Lack of Attention to Detail

A lack of attention to detail often comes across as carelessness on the child's behalf. They may not attend to what is being explained in class or what you tell them to do at home. When they take on a task, they will often not complete it or leave out important aspects that the job entails. Their brains have such a need for novel stimuli that slowing down to see something through to fruition feels torturous.

Struggling to Pay Attention

It is usually in class that their inability to focus on their school work or the lessons presented becomes evident. However, this behavior also surfaces in more informal situations, such as play during recess. Your child may be unable to commit themselves to any task, especially those requiring their attention for more extended periods.

Losing Themselves in Thought

It is typical for a child with ADHD to drift off, completely lost in thought. During these moments, they won't be able to focus and might not even hear you talking to them. Understandably, this can be a huge concern for parents and teachers alike.

An Inability to Follow Instructions

A child's inability to listen to instructions is closely linked with the previous point. This often happens due to them being lost in their thoughts. As they haven't been listening to the instructions given to them, or struggle with the working memory required to repeat said instructions, following this guidance is quite a challenge to them. However, it is not only instructions that present a challenge for the ADHD child. Rules can become a similar issue, as children with ADHD often can't focus long enough to grasp what was communicated to them or have the impulse control to resist rule-breaking urges.

Struggling to Present Their Solutions

While the previous point states that children with ADHD often struggle to follow instructions, this doesn't equate to their having an inability to come to the correct answers in class. An ADHD child is perfectly capable of finding solutions. However, they lack the ability to present how they came to the answers they have. A person with ADHD's train of thought runs on "superspeed." Our minds jump from topic to topic following a series of connected clues that are seemingly random to outsiders. Because of this, we are often innovative thinkers. However, this mental flexibility combined with memory difficulties means that people with ADHD often can't backtrack their thinking to explain it to others, leaving them frustrated and unable to speak up in class.

Zero Organization Skills

While it may not necessarily be that your child comes across as entirely incapable of any level of organization, it can undoubtedly often feels that way to parents. You may have to constantly remind your child to get into—and again out of—the bath, brush their teeth, or complete any other routine activity as they struggle to organize and manage their time. This inability often leads to mood swings and can prompt severe anger outbursts.

You Have to Remind Them Constantly of Everything

One of the most exhausting tasks of the child's parents can be to constantly remind the child to keep track of their belongings and time, set their goals, complete tasks, and basically anything else they must remember.

This is particularly necessary because people with ADHD often cannot feel the passage of time, and therefore, even when they are aware that something needs to be done to a schedule, they will need external reminders of the deadline's approach.

They Forget Things

The need for reminders also occurs because forgetfulness is a pretty common trait among those who have ADHD. They can forget anything from where they left their possessions, the work they need to complete, and their duties at home. In adulthood, this forgetfulness can become an even more significant concern, as it is common for adults with ADHD to forget to pay their bills or go to scheduled medical appointments.

They Avoid Tasks Demanding Concentration

As they struggle to maintain their focus, it is understandable that a person with ADHD portrays a resistance towards tasks demanding their focus for long periods, and they will try to avoid these tasks. However, this will only apply to subjects in which the individual has no interest. When their interest is piqued, a child with ADHD can have seeming superhuman focus.

HYPERACTIVITY

This one is in the name itself—attention deficit *hyperactivity* disorder. This is usually the symptom of ADHD that is the most misunderstood in children. Hyperactive behavior can very easily be mistaken as being "naughty," when the truth is that it is very unlikely that your child is trying to misbehave.

ADHD minds have to be entertained and have fun at all times. While adults may throw this energy into their passion, children have only one way of getting it out: playing. Hyperactive kids seem to always be moving. They need the next game, task, distraction, or activity like they need air. Before attributing this kind of behavior to ADHD, however, your medical professional will first rule out other possible causes, such as emotional concerns and stress which can cause hyperactive behavior in minors. Additionally, your child may be facing other challenges—such as learning disabilities and vision problems—that might, in turn, be causing hyperactive behavior. Your doctor will determine whether your child's behavior is normal for their development stage.

As part of a conventional approach to determining an ADHD diagnosis, your doctor will have to confirm a minimum of six symptoms of hyperactivity, which might include the following:

- Your child enjoys climbing, jumping, playing, or roughhousing, even when they have been told it's time to play quietly. They may continue playing rambunctiously even if all the kids around them play quietly. They are constantly on the move, running without reason or end. You'll see them getting up from their seat to climb over furniture or jump around. They take risks: Young kids could run into the street without looking for oncoming cars while teens might take up smoking, for instance.
- They have no patience and can't wait their turn. Your child will blurt out comments and interrupt conversations. They just don't have the patience to wait until they have a turn to speak or check if the environment is safe. They need to get their ideas out quickly before they forget them.
- They have trouble sitting still, constantly fidgeting, tapping their feet or hands, or playing with random objects to pass the time. If your child is forced to sit quietly, they may become moody and restless.

- Your child always seems to be in a rush. When doing important things requiring patience, your child runs through tasks like *The Flash*, leaving a multitude of half-finished projects in their wake. Alternatively, you may notice that your child spends a lot of time on a seemingly simple task. For your child, making the bed may take half an hour, as they insist there is no wrinkle in sight.
- Your child never calms down. They are constantly on the move, doing something, on their way to doing something, or planning to do something. They need the thrill of new stimuli to engage their busy brain.
- When your child is busy with tasks, you may notice that they make careless mistakes. This may be a result of rushing through the task, or it may be a result of their inability to focus thoroughly enough to do the job accurately. Not having patience can cause conflict at school or with friends. As adults, they may find it exceptionally hard to sit still, as they constantly appear on the go. Therefore, sitting through meetings can be a real pain for them. However, if they've learned techniques to manage their inability to sit still, people with ADHD can

reduce the impact of their symptoms. We can teach our kids how to do that, as well.

IMPULSIVITY

Individuals with ADHD have a tough time controlling their impulses. Once their brain has an idea, they simply have to do it. Sometimes, it's like their brain goes on auto-pilot, and they do a thing before they have thought it through. Other times, they cannot get the thing off their mind, drawing their attention away from "more important" matters. Until they do the thing, they will be obsessing over it.

Impulsivity can present in the following ways:

- Your child may unintentionally interrupt a lot. Because your child has something to say, they may not notice that someone else is speaking. The most important thing to your child at that moment is getting that thought out of their mouth before they forget it.
- Your child may blurt out things without thinking. This can be in the form of irrelevant or even inappropriate remarks or questions. Your child has no sense of the right time or place to say, do, or ask something. They simply act on their first thought.

- Your child often does things without thinking them through. You may watch other children scope out a jungle gym before tackling it head-on. Meanwhile, your child is on their third attempt as they jump into it with no forethought. For children, this may lead to many injuries; as adults, repercussions may come in the form of an empty bank account, employment termination, a criminal record, or worse. Therefore, impulsivity, in particular, should be mentioned to a mental healthcare professional so that coping mechanisms may be learned before long-term real-world consequences have the chance to take effect.
- Your child often misbehaves, even if they know better. Even if your child knows they can't have cookies before supper, once their mind thinks of cookies, they can't stop themselves from snagging a few and running to their room like a tiny, evil genius.
- Your child often has trouble waiting, taking turns, or sharing. If your child wants to do something, they want to do it now. They don't want to wait. They don't want to be interrupted. They don't want to pause.
- Your child often has emotional outbursts. Impulsivity not only relates to behavior but also

refers to emotions too. Impulsivity makes it challenging for people with ADHD to identify their feelings and understand why they are feeling them—a symptom known as *alexithymia*. Instead of consciously noticing their emotions and choosing how to respond, people with ADHD are usually stuck feeling the first emotion that surfaces, often pretty intensely. This can lead to a severe lack of self-control or regularly losing their temper. If this happens regularly in your home, you may find yourself wondering if you did something to cause it: Don't worry, other parents think that about their kids, too. Rest assured, it is highly unlikely that you are your child's stumbling block. The challenge that a child with ADHD is facing is that inability to control their behavior, attention, and activities naturally. Therefore, the more parents are familiar with what causes their child to behave in a specific manner, the more effective their approach will be in addressing the concern.

BOYS, GIRLS, AND ADHD

You may have a girl; you may have a boy. You may have both. Perhaps, your child doesn't wish to ascribe to the gender binary whatsoever. Nevertheless, it is often difficult to avoid the "gender discussion" when discussing mental or physical health issues. ADHD is no different—there is a vast difference in how ADHD presents in young boys and girls. Because of this, there is also a vast difference in the diagnoses of ADHD in boys and girls.

CDC data and statistics relating to ADHD in 2021 show that boys are more than twice as likely to be diagnosed with ADHD. This information indicates that 13% of boys are likely to be diagnosed with ADHD, while the percentage for girls is only 6% (National Center for Birth Defects and Developmental Disabilities, 2022). Why is that?

To begin with, ADHD in boys tends to be very "obvious," meaning many symptoms are external. Boys with ADHD are usually loud, energetic, rambunctious, and sometimes destructive. On the opposite side of the spectrum, ADHD in girls often presents with mostly internal symptoms. Girls are much better at "hiding," or "masking," their ADHD than boys are. They tend to be held to higher standards of "respectability" from a young age and are, therefore, much more likely to try to correct their symptoms and behavior to fit the social norm.

Boys are also more likely to be referred for ADHD diagnoses and treatment than girls are. You can imagine the reason for that: Because boys' symptoms are much more external than girls', this also means that they are more disruptive and noticeable. Boys with ADHD are likelier to be disruptive in class, start fights, or be loud. This sort of behavior is a red flag for teachers who are on the lookout for children who might be struggling with any mental disorders or neurodivergence.

On the other hand, girls are less likely to be so external or disruptive with their behavior. Girls with ADHD are much more likely to present with symptoms such as daydreaming, forgetting or losing things, or being messy or chatty. However, these symptoms can be—and often are—dismissed as "typical girl" behavior. All little girls like to talk and daydream all day, right?

Daydreaming and being talkative are not hugely disruptive behaviors. This means that girls with ADHD are less likely to be on a teacher's radar for conditions like ADHD. Girls are much less likely to be noticed to be struggling or impaired. Therefore, they are less likely to be referred for diagnosis or treatment.

Moreover, boys are more likely to present the "typical" ADHD symptoms that parents and teachers are aware of. Girls, on the other hand, are more likely to show the lesser-known but still relevant symptoms of ADHD. Thus, it's less likely for a parent or teacher to recognize these symptoms of ADHD in girls.

However, the ways that ADHD introduces struggles into the life of those with it are much the same. Boys and girls alike will struggle with motivation, their perception of time, a lack of organization, and forgetfulness.

So, how can we close the gap between the number of diagnosed boys and girls? We can start by becoming familiar with the internal and external symptoms and signs of ADHD.

External symptoms of ADHD may include

- impulsivity
- regular bouts of "acting out"
- excessive talking
- regularly interrupting others
- physical aggression—such as pushing, roughhousing, throwing toys, punching tables, etc.
- hyperactivity
- inattentiveness

Internal symptoms of ADHD may include

- having a challenging time focusing and paying attention
- difficulty listening to or following instructions
- avoiding tasks or activities that require a lot of quiet, sitting still, or paying close attention
- withdrawn behavior
- forgetfulness
- difficulty keeping their surroundings and possessions orderly and tidy
- often making avoidable mistakes due to a lack of concentration
- extreme difficulty with starting or transitioning to a new activity or task
- verbal aggression—such as name-calling, taunting, swearing, etc.

Many of these symptoms can lead to—or be perceived as—intellectual impairment or difficulty achieving academic ventures.

If left untreated, more internal symptoms may appear:

- depression
- stress
- anxiety
- urges to self-harm

- low self-esteem
- self-criticism

When reading through these symptoms, please remember that each child is unique and will experience their own neurotype differently. Not all boys with ADHD will be rowdy and destructive; not all girls will be withdrawn and daydreamy. These are all symptoms of ADHD, and they can present in boys and girls without regard to gender.

Please remember that these general gender-based trends do not mean that there are no boys who have internal symptoms or no girls who have external symptoms. Anyone can present with either one or the other, or perhaps, even a mix of the two. So, it is good to monitor your child's behavior carefully. What's essential, in the meantime, is for us to destroy the idea that ADHD is a boy's disorder.

As we get to know our children, and the more we understand their personalities, what makes them feel good, and what doesn't, the more we can teach them how to use everything they have to their advantage. To be able to change something for the better, we must first see what we can work with. So, when keeping an eye out for ADHD in your children, be sure to watch for those internal symptoms just as well as the external ones.

Be careful, though: Inattention in children, for example, is not always due to ADHD. Many factors can cause such behavior—for instance, tiredness, chronic illness, or the impact of a learning disability. It is vital for the health of your child that you do not just dismiss their behavior, as it can have medical implications too. Tiredness is often the result of sleep-disordered breathing. This is a medical concern more prevalent in obese children and kids with extra-large tonsils or adenoids. Another medical concern causing tiredness is pediatric hypothyroidism which can be improved with the correct medication.

Sometimes, constant tiredness is just the outcome of changed sleeping habits, or your child not getting as much sleep as needed. These causes can be addressed by making changes to their bedtime. Parents need to consider all the possible reasons behind their child's inattentive behavior to find the best treatment options. The answer may be ADHD alone, it could be something else, or it can be ADHD alongside other compounding conditions—as we will discuss in the next section.

ADHD, AMONG OTHER THINGS

ADHD is often not an isolated disorder. It is important to know the common comorbidities that exist and how to identify them.

The most common among these disorders are

- oppositional defiant disorder (ODD)
- conduct disorder (CD)
- learning disorders—such as dyslexia, dyscalculia, or dysgraphia
- anxiety
- depression

It often happens that in addition to ADHD, another condition is present. That's why it's essential that if you suspect your child has ADHD, your mental healthcare provider screens them for other conditions as well.

I know it can be a daunting process to consider yet another diagnosis that your child may need to pursue, but remember that all information is good information. By understanding our child's needs, we can meet them. We start from the roots to the leaves.

Oppositional Defiant Disorder

Approximately, 40% of children diagnosed with ADHD may also develop ODD (*The ADHD and ODD link in children*, 2020). Young children often develop ODD as an unhealthy coping mechanism for the challenges associated with ADHD. Symptoms of ODD may include

- chronic aggression
- a tendency to ignore orders or requests
- persistent arguing (even when unnecessary)
- frequent emotional or aggressive outbursts
- engaging in intentionally disruptive or irritating behavior
- easily losing their temper
- using others as scapegoats for their own bad behavior

The article states that about 50% of children diagnosed with ODD will outgrow the disorder by the age of eight (*The ADHD and ODD link in children*, 2020). However, if ODD is left untreated, it has the potential to evolve into conduct disorder (CD).

Conduct Disorder

Children may be diagnosed with CD if they show aggressive behavior or extreme violation of rules.

Conduct disorder can potentially lead to lawbreaking and/or arrest. CD may include behavior such as

- crossing serious boundaries—such as stealing, running away, missing curfew, underage drinking, etc.
- showing physical aggression towards objects, people, or animals—such as throwing things, punching walls, abusing animals, etc.
- excessive—or even pathological—lying
- committing theft or property damage

As you can likely tell, allowing your child with CD to go untreated may end badly for their well-being, safety, and future, as well as those around them.

Learning Disorders

Behavior disorders are not the only conditions that may come along with ADHD. As you can imagine, ADHD massively impacts the academic life of those afflicted. Not being able to maintain concentration is not an attribute that lends itself to a successful academic career. But, beyond that, ADHD may also come alongside even more academic challenges, such as learning disorders.

It's important to remember that learning disorders do not always affect the actual intelligence of a child.

Learning disorders merely add a challenge when trying to apply their intellect to something. Learning disorders include

- dyslexia: difficulty with processing written language in the form of difficulty reading, writing, and specifically spelling
- dyscalculia: difficulty with mathematical abilities
- dysgraphia: difficulty with handwriting in the form of having illegible handwriting or taking very long to write things down

Having ADHD in combination with one of these learning disorders can make academic success extremely difficult for those afflicted, even more so if left untreated. Accessibility and alternative strategies are required to give children with ADHD and/or learning disabilities an equal shot at academic success.

As mentioned earlier, learning disorders and ADHD are not determinants of your child's intelligence. Your child's intelligence is most likely to develop the same way it would have otherwise. However, applying this intelligence—particularly in relation to strict educational goals and assessments—becomes a lot more difficult for them.

Left untreated, this can lead not only to academic failure but also to low self-esteem due to this failure. Being in constant trouble at school can also lead to poor mental health and anxiety or depression.

Anxiety and Depression

We have all heard of depression and anxiety. Hell, many of us have experienced (or are experiencing) it firsthand. It's not difficult to imagine how a disorder like ADHD—especially if left untreated—can lead someone to anxiety or depression. For myself and many others, the constant additional struggles can take an extreme mental toll.

The direct impact of ADHD on the afflicted's emotional state is also not often discussed. It is not usually acknowledged that those with ADHD suffer from rejection-sensitive dysphoria (RSD): an extreme emotional reaction when experiencing or perceiving rejection or criticism from loved ones and other emotional conditions (*Rejection Sensitive Dysphoria (RSD), 2022*). There is a significant emotional impact when being reprimanded for something they cannot control, failing to do something they truly want to—and know they can—do, or getting stuck in ADHD paralysis when they have important obligations.

Often, this emotional overload can manifest in anxiety or depression. Anxiety can include

- separation anxiety: developing an attachment to loved ones to the point of being afraid or agitated when away from them
- social anxiety: having difficulty with and becoming anxious when in large crowds or meeting strangers
- general anxiety: distress that can be very easily triggered by an array of different things

Unfortunately, many people dismiss anxiety as a mental disorder, claiming that since everyone worries and has fears that they must deal with, anxious thinking is the norm. However, any behavior becomes disordered when it interferes with your everyday life, well-being, or responsibility. It inhibits you from being able to perform the way that someone without the disorder might.

Depression is another of those disorders that can severely impact the lives of those afflicted, despite a certain level of public dismissal. "Depression," as a term, is used liberally in everyday language, even for the mildest sadnesses. However, depression is a severe and ever-prevalent mental disorder. It is very dangerous to develop as it comes with many risks. Those with depression can become a danger to themselves and others if left untreated.

Symptoms of depression may include

- feelings of sadness or hopelessness that are constant or frequent
- losing interest in hobbies, passions, or fun things
- loss of appetite
- trouble focusing
- frequent feelings of being worthless or useless

So, how can you tell when your child's lack of focus is ADHD-related or depression-related? Those with ADHD have difficulty focusing, especially on things that do not interest them. You may notice that your child will lack focus when forced to do something they perceive as boring but perk up at the mention of a topic of interest to them. However, you can identify when that lack of focus is coming from a place of depression if your child struggles to focus, even on things they would generally find fun, engaging, or stimulating. Children who look, behave, and act more or less typically are unlikely to be very ill. A healthy child generally has a good appetite and gets a full night's sleep. They will also have plenty of energy and natural curiosity in their surroundings and normally act appropriately for their age.

Mental disorders in children are often determined by how they behave and express themselves. Other signs can be seen in how they manage their emotions, get through the events that they experience, and mesh with others during the day. If their behavior causes regular disruptions during the day at home, school, or during fun activities, they may be dealing with a disorder of some kind. The sooner you can identify and address these concerns, the greater impact you'll have on improving their future.

For many reasons, those with ADHD should be screened for other conditions. Receiving a diagnosis and the appropriate treatment as soon as possible can make a world of difference in your child's future. Being mentally supported and healthy during childhood means reaching developmental and emotional milestones, learning healthy social skills, and coping with problems. Mentally healthy children have a positive quality of life and can function well at home, in school, and in their communities.

ARE THEY NAUGHTY, OR IS IT ADHD?

Looking back, I remember that my parents' attitude to my behavior was to disregard every symptom, labeling everything under the word "naughtiness." Nowadays, many parents have more access to information and can avoid bringing such stereotypes and stigmas into their houses. Yet, it can still happen. It's easy to rely on an inaccurate label when you do not know what else to do. Then, the go-to response is, "they're just naughty," or maybe even "way too naughty."

But at the same time, you can't help but be hurt, as a parent, to see them struggling, not succeeding. It's hard to admit that moments of joy and peace in the house are rare. When a child has poor grades at school, doesn't tidy up their room, won't help you with any tasks at home, is absent from school, or acts aggressively, it can feel like they just don't respect you or anything around them. But how do they, the child, feel when all these things happen?

I can tell you how it was for me and how I see my own experiences reflected in the children I have worked with over the years. Childhood years go like this: At home, there is always an argument based on what wasn't done well. At school, you experience a continuous feeling of helplessness, and among friends, you are forever the "different" one. Adults, yes, ask you to be more careful, more attentive, to not forget, to stick to school, not to lie, and to be more organized. The kids try, too. They try, but—especially when you have ADHD—it doesn't work out the first time. You need a lot of practice and a lot of patience. And, when you feel that your parents' demands sound more like a reproach than an "I notice that you are struggling. Let's think about a solution together," you can only assume that they expect the worst from you. You worry that they will take revenge, thinking that you don't love them.

I sincerely believe that nothing in life could be more painful than thinking that your parents do not care about you. But the attitude in which parents do or say things has the potential to change everything. When you are about to give directions, pause and take a second look. In front of you, sits a fidgeting child. In their heart of hearts, they want to do the task at hand, but their brain is making it very difficult for them to focus. There is a bird outside, and everything inside them tells them to play with it. They know that you are disappointed in them. They know that you think they are naughty. So, they try their best to make you proud. But they still can't focus. Their legs are itchy, their ears are ringing, and now, they are hungry.

They might start talking about the bird outside. If they are talking about it, maybe that itch in their head will be scratched. But they should be doing the activity. At one point, they become so frustrated that they throw their things to the floor and run to the other side of the room. They do this because acting out feels better than sitting still and being unable to do the task at hand. This "naughty" child is struggling. This "naughty" child is trying their best to counteract the way their mind naturally works.

The difference between misbehaving and ADHD is that children with ADHD show symptoms such as aggression and frustration over a longer period, which may eventually lead to problems in a child's ability to function at school, at home, and with friends.

"But, with self-discipline, they can get over the distractions, right?" Also wrong—or at least, oversimplified. Inside the mind of someone with ADHD, the concept of self-discipline is complicated. We might be able to acknowledge how we could implement self-discipline —"Okay, you can play with the birdy outside once you've built the blocks. All you have to do is focus for five minutes, then you can go have fun." However, our thoughts soon run away with us—"Wait, why do that when I can go have fun now? What's the worst that can happen if I don't play with the blocks right this second?

What if the bird flies away?" Of course, this example is highly simplified for the sake of explanation, but the concept remains. It is not a child's fault if their mind works differently from everyone else's. It does not make them naughty or unruly. It means they need help to overcome the extra challenges that make even the simplest of tasks more difficult for them.

There is, however, a way to tell whether a child's behavior is caused by ADHD or by naughtiness:

- Duration of behavior: Naughty behavior often doesn't persist for long. A poor night's rest, a sore stomach, or even mom and dad fighting can cause an otherwise calm and collected child to fidget, become irritable, and be unable to concentrate. However, if several days or weeks have passed, and the child is consistently restless, hyperactive, and inattentive, they very well may have ADHD.
- Environmental factors: As mentioned before, many things can cause different behaviors. A child may have said something rude simply in retaliation to rudeness from another child. It doesn't have to signify that anything more permanent is impacting them. A child may be aggressive if their parents exhibit aggressive behavior at home. A child may behave

hyperactively to gain the attention of otherwise unaware parents or peers. Consider a child's home and school environments before labeling them with bad behavior or ADHD. If there is no apparent explanation available at home or with their peers, and they continue to show these symptoms, they may have ADHD.

- Context: A child may be labeled as naughty and aggressive when the truth is that they are dealing with a school bully, and they are acting in the only way that feels safe currently. Likewise, the child may be labeled as inattentive, while the truth of the matter shows that they have had three *Pop-Tarts* for lunch and are on a sugar rush.
- Results: A child may struggle with a disorder if you notice their behavior disrupts and affects their lives. If their interrupting keeps them from making friends, their aggression is causing them to hurt themselves, or their inattentiveness is causing them to receive bad grades, they may be struggling with a disorder.

A good rule of thumb would be to monitor a child's behavior over time rather than analyzing isolated events. Generally, if a specific behavior continues for more than six months, and no environmental factors might be the cause, it's best to seek a mental health professional.

Ultimately, a lot of unusual childhood behavior called attention-seeking, and that doesn't always have to be a bad thing. Generally, if a child is seeking attention, it means they need it. They need help, or they need support. It's important to always look deeper than face value. Even if a child does not have a disorder and is acting out, it's our responsibility, as adults, to look further into why they are behaving the way they are.

Bad behavior can be a signal for teachers and for parents. It can be indicative of a mental health disorder, but it may also be a sign that a child is dealing with something with which they are not fully qualified to cope. This might signal a bad home environment, a bully, or even some form of abuse. It is heartbreaking, but the truth is that not every bout of bad behavior is superficial. Occasionally, and unfortunately, a child's bad behavior could be a call for help.

Seeking answers is always helpful. When you're a parent, life's not just about you anymore. So, in the parent role, what is the point of allowing these negative feelings in your life? Does it help you or your child with anything? Or would you both be better served by seeking truth and treatment?

When your child's behavior isn't improving, it can leave you feeling frustrated, embarrassed, stressed, and disrespected. Feeling this way is normal, as you don't know yet that your child's behavior is not a reflection of your parenting. Only once your child has a positive diagnosis can you start working on finding solutions and ways to best manage their behavior.

POSITIVE PARENTING TIP

Six months can be a long time to accurately monitor and track your child's behavior. How can you be expected to remember their behavior from seven days ago? It might be even worse if you're a teacher trying to monitor many little ones and stay on track. It may be worth downloading a mood or behavior-tracking application on your phone. Having a record of your child's mood and behavior will give you a good overview of the situation. Should you need to see a mental health professional, it will be invaluable to their diagnosis.

Linking in with your child's school can also help you to analyze patterns in their behavior across different environments. This is made easier if you have the opportunity to choose an inclusive and accessible, collaboration-oriented school for your child, to begin with. The right school placement is crucial (as we will discuss further in Chapter 10). Parents should consider the following when looking at schools:

- Does school management understand the impact of ADHD on the lives of those in school? Determine the understanding of managing your child's ADHD, as the culture of acceptance must be supported from the top.
- Does the school offer training to teachers to expand their understanding of ADHD?
- Is the school actively involved with a special educational needs coordinator (SENCO), and does the SENCO ensure that all staff are familiar with the needs of children with ADHD? What is the staff's approach toward managing the school environment to accommodate your child's needs?

Find out if there is pastoral support at your child's school, allowing students to develop trusting and sound relationships with some of the teachers. Some questions you should include when consulting with any school regarding your child would also be whether they teach social and well-being skills at the school and how important they consider this as part of their curriculum. When it comes to the curriculum, it is also useful to know if the school empowers all children to develop control over their responses and whether they aim to increase awareness of the individual needs of children and support those specific needs.

Lastly, a school that offers safe spaces where your child can chill out or just take a break when hyperactive without being reprimanded would be preferred.

For teachers, finding a simple and quick way of tracking a child's moods and behaviors can save them a lot of stress. Assigning a color to each student and a symbol to different behaviors you are looking for can be a quick way to jot down which student is exhibiting noteworthy behaviors.

Finding the right school for your child is crucial. A few things you need to consider when considering schools for your child are whether the staff understands how it works when your child needs to take medication and whether the school offers support to the parents or maybe even recommends support groups outside of the school structure. Also, determine how often the school will give feedback on your child's general performance and progress and how they do this.

2

MOMMY, DADDY, CAN YOU SEE ME?

It is the hope of each and every individual on this planet to be understood by those we love. Many parents hope to be able to understand their children with the aim of supporting them through thick and thin. Understanding your child is the first step in developing a plan to help them with whatever challenges they may face.

The first step in this process is considering how their minds work to interpret the world around them. Unfortunately, for many parents, children—especially children with ADHD—are not fully capable of putting into words how they feel. Furthermore, a child with ADHD has no way of knowing that how their mind works is not how a neurotypical mind might work. So, as adults, it's up to us to more fully comprehend and analyze behaviors and emotions to fill in the gaps. For this reason, it can be helpful to put ourselves in the shoes of a few individuals with ADHD. This will not only deepen your understanding of the condition but also allow you to empathize with your child about their struggles, encouraging them to vocalize their emotions.

CASE STUDIES

Abby's Story

Abigail has just started kindergarten. She loves it. She has so many new friends to talk to, the teacher is fun and cool, and there are lots of toys to play with. Sometimes, Abby wishes she had eight arms like an octopus, so she could play with all the toys at once.

But Abigail doesn't always get to play with toys. Sometimes, she has to pay attention and stuff. Sometimes, she has to sit still while the teacher speaks, and then she has to do work. She usually doesn't mind doing the work. It's fun work.

But sometimes, Abby struggles. Sometimes, the work is very boring. She'd rather be playing with the toys. All her friends seem happy to wait until their work is done to play with the toys. Meanwhile, Abby can't keep her eyes off them. They're so bright and colorful, and they're practically begging for her to go over and play with them.

When she hears the teacher talking, it's as if the bright colors from the toys block her ears. It's difficult to hear what the teacher says because Abby wishes she would say that it's toy time.

She can get herself to listen to the teacher every now and then. But the teacher talks so slowly! First, she must pick the blue crayon and color in the sky. Then, she must pick the green crayon and color in the grass. But Abby can see the whole picture and knows what colors go where. She gets in trouble for coloring in her picture before everyone else has started.

"The sun is not supposed to be purple, Abigail. You need to listen more closely," says the teacher. But all the other children's drawings aren't even finished yet; hers is already colored in, and now she can go play, right?

Then comes nap time. Abby *hates* nap time. She often becomes inconsolable and very rowdy, making it difficult for the other children. Nap time is too quiet and boring! Nobody is allowed to speak. And when Abby is trying her best to settle down, she gets in trouble for scratching every itch and shifting into a comfortable position every three seconds. She can't go to sleep if she's uncomfortable, and she is always uncomfortable.

Abby's favorite part of the day is when she gets to play outside. According to her teachers, a bomb could go off next to Abby when she's playing with the flowers and she wouldn't notice. For a child who struggles to pay attention, she sure can focus on something as unimportant as flowers.

What will the teachers do with her?

Jonah's Story

Jonah is just scraping by in school. School used to be tolerable, if not fun. But lately, ever since he's actually had to start studying in order to pass, it's become unbearable. When did coloring in pages and simple math flash cards become lackluster? It was easier—well, not easy but not nearly as impossible as it feels now—to focus in a room full of others when all he had to do was match the cow to the glass of milk.

Now, when he has to do equations and know what a metaphor is, the other children in the class are walking, breathing distractions that he can't block out. Stacy has a constant foot tap that drives him up the wall. He swears that it echoes off the walls and directly into the center of his brain to make it rattle like the toy of an upset toddler. Gary is a great friend, but his constant whispering makes Jonah feel like his skin is on fire.

The papers on his desk—that he ought to be paying attention to—feel like they are flying around his head. The need to pay attention to them is taking up all his focus. So much so that he can't focus on them. He doesn't think anyone would understand if he tried to explain it. How can you be so worried about focusing that you can't focus?

As each day goes by, and he falls further and further behind, that need to focus continues to grow more and more urgent, but also more and more daunting. Because now it's not just studying; it's also having to catch up with everything he's missed. Tests are getting closer and closer, and he feels like he's at the bottom of a huge mountain with no damn footholds for him to climb.

"You just need to focus. You need to remove every source of distraction and force yourself to do the work, Jonah." That's his dad's advice. But how does Jonah explain that there is no removing *every* source of distraction? Can he remove the walls in his room because the pattern is entrancing? Can he remove the ceiling fan because it squeaks? Can he remove the heat because it makes him sweat and itch?

But Jonah tries. He absolutely forces himself to study. He berates himself. He talks down to himself. He verbally and mentally abuses himself in order to get even one page of studying in. And through all that, he still can't focus properly. How useless and worthless he feels he must be. It can't be *that* difficult to focus, can it?

Melanie's Story

Melanie has a very important book report due in a week. This should be a piece of cake. She starts on Monday morning by making a game plan. Successful people make game plans. She'll have to reread the book to ensure all the information is fresh in her mind. If she reads 52 pages a day, she'll be done by Thursday. But, she should make notes as she reads so that she doesn't forget anything.

But her notebook is running low on empty pages. She'll need to buy a new one. So, she'll have to go to the store. What else does she need at the store? She goes to check her room. It's a mess. She won't know what she needs if she doesn't know what she already has. It's time to do some spring cleaning and organizing.

She'll start by her desk since it's the most important at the moment. Her desk is covered in clothes. She thinks they're clean. She has to fold them and pack them away. But if she's busy with her clothes, she might as well do a load of laundry. Her mom has been telling her to do it for a few days. Oh, her mom has also been telling her to tidy up her bookshelf. She's busy cleaning up her room anyway, so maybe she should start with the bookshelf.

That's where her new novel went! She'd forgotten she bought it. Maybe she could listen to an audiobook as she cleans. That would be a great way to multitask.

By Tuesday morning, Melanie has not read her first 52 pages nor has she bought herself a new notebook. Her room is even more of a mess. But she finished that new novel. It was great—five stars. Okay, she can still get back on track. She just needs to read 104 pages to make up for the previous day. Her game plan can still work.

Oh, she never finished drawing up her game plan. Where did she put it? She'll have to start again. Okay, a good book report is well thought out. She should draw up a mindmap of topics to cover. But, she needs to read the book first. Wait, doesn't this book have a movie adaptation? She can watch the movie to start planning and read the book for more specific details.

Yes, she found three movie adaptations. Should she watch the oldest or the newest one? Maybe, she should watch all three. Perhaps, the differences in the movies could be a talking point.

On Wednesday morning, Melanie has not yet read her 104 pages. She only watched the first half hour of the oldest adaptation—it was boring. Instead, she found herself watching the first season of *Friends*. She had forgotten how much she enjoyed that show. It's Wednesday now, and she's falling behind. Her mom said she'd take her to the store to get her notebook today. That's good.

What can she do in the meantime? She gets home at two, and her mom said she'd fetch her at four. Well, that's not enough time to do anything at all. She'll just have to wait for her mom before doing anything else.

The trip to the store took longer than she thought. Her mom wanted to do all their grocery shopping. Now, Melanie is starting to get stressed. She's supposed to finish reading the book by Thursday. She's determined to stick to her game plan. She skips dinner and only goes to bed at 4 a.m., but she manages to read the entire novel.

Great! She feels great! She's back on track. But on Thursday, she is exhausted because of her all-nighter. She can't keep herself awake, let alone do the mindmap and planning for the report. She'll have to do it over the weekend.

But Fridays are her "chill" days. Her mom and dad are very strict about her getting a day of rest so she doesn't become overwhelmed and overburnt. She gets nothing done on Friday. How is she going to write the entire book report in two days?

Saturday morning, Melanie starts her book report, finally. She forgot to take notes, though. So, every 10 minutes, she opens her book to read the entire chapter she is referring to. But, she just read the book. Rereading it is unbearably boring. If she continues, she might go into a reading slump. She's struggling to focus. She needs a break.

Before she knows it, it's Saturday evening.

Melanie's Sunday is spent in a crying mess, writing as fast as she can to get the report done. Her body is on fire as she forces herself to sit and finish the entire book report before doing anything else. Everything is itchy. The silence is deafening, but listening to music is distracting.

One a.m. comes, and Melanie puts her pen down. She smiles. She did it. She is so proud of herself. She promises herself that she won't ever put herself in this position again.

On Monday morning, her science teacher announces that they have a project due in a week. Awesome. She'll have to start with a game plan.

ADHD, WITH EMPHASIS ON DISORDER

The word "disorder" often invokes stereotypical and stigmatized images of psychiatric wards, but realistically, this is not accurate. The APA defines a mental disorder as a syndrome that

- causes significant disruption in cognition, behavior, and emotion.
- usually affects the afflicted's work, school, and social relationships (n.d.).

So, according to this definition, can ADHD be categorized as a disorder? Absolutely, it can. Let's take a look at why.

Cognition

When examining the cognitive performance—attention, hyperactivity, impulsivity, and timing—of a group of children aged 6–11 years old, studies found children with ADHD performed at a level comparable to the results of neurotypical children who were 1–3 years younger than them (Low, 2022). In fact, when testing hyperactivity specifically, that age gap was even larger. Therefore, when reflecting back on the definition of a disorder we might ask, *Does ADHD disrupt one's cognition?* Yes, it does.

Behavior

As previously mentioned, a large factor in how professionals diagnose children with ADHD is their behavior. Professionals actively examine the differences in behavior between neurotypical children and children with ADHD.

Therefore, the symptoms of ADHD outline the ways in which it affects a child's behavior. ADHD causes restlessness, impulsivity, aggression, talkativeness, etc. ADHD can make it so that certain behaviors turn into unbreakable habits while others become impossible to perform.

For children with ADHD, a certain task can be the absolute most important thing to them. In this case, they will hyper-focus on it, neglecting other important tasks like hygiene, eating, or sleeping. On the other hand, they can also find certain tasks to be simply impossible to perform. This could be due to sensory overload or a lack of engagement, but they would literally do *anything* else.

Does ADHD disrupt one's behavior? Absolutely.

Work

To be successful in the working environment requires a particular set of skills. In this case, I am not talking about the five years of experience and a GPA of 4.0. No, here, I am talking about certain skills that *every* type of job asks for, regardless of the academic or experience requirements: To get and keep a job, you must be able to manage your time. You must be able to prioritize tasks properly and you must have an eye for details. You must be able to follow directions, work within a plan, and pay attention to the rules and directions given.

For people with ADHD, many of those skills are simply out of the question. People with ADHD have immense difficulty with

- management of time and resources
- prioritizing
- remembering details
- following instructions
- paying attention

The typical working environment is not designed to help people with ADHD be productive. People with ADHD struggle with sitting behind a desk all day or doing the same task over and over again. So, yes, ADHD definitely impacts one's work life.

School

It's no secret that children with ADHD have trouble in school. Between struggles with academic achievement, behavioral issues, and possible learning disabilities, school can be a monumental mountain for children with ADHD to climb.

Children with ADHD are more likely to get reprimanded for not paying attention or disrupting the class. They are also more likely to have learning disabilities which make academic achievement all the more difficult. The symptoms that children with ADHD exhibit at school can be mistaken as "laziness" or "rebellion" when, in actual fact, they are struggling to reach the same level as their peers.

Reaching "normal" levels of concentration takes so much focus that there is little energy left for the actual task. In other words, children with ADHD can be focusing so hard on focusing that they can't focus on what they're supposed to be focused on. Staying engaged takes constant vigilance, reminders, and reprimands and is extremely tolling on the mind. This is because people with ADHD have many executive function deficits; things like initiation, focus, effort, emotions, memory, and action functions are extremely difficult for them.

Moreover, these academic frustrations can be exacerbated by having problems with social interactions that can play a big part in their struggles at school. As we will discuss further below, an inability to make friends or communicate effectively can make school feel like a big and lonely place. Thus, can we say that ADHD disrupts the school life of those with the condition? Yes.

Social Relationships

Being able to make and maintain friendships is a skill that many people naturally have. Of course, it is also a skill that many people lack. Some people are not naturally charismatic and have to try harder to make and maintain friendships. ADHD does not change this fact.

Very often, children with ADHD are very charismatic and personable. Their tendency to change topics abruptly is age-appropriate and might even be seen as endearing. However, as these children grow and potentially face increasing criticism for their behavior, it is very possible for ADHD to cause rejection sensitivity, a tendency to isolate, and low self-esteem in those afflicted. It can be difficult to initiate friendships when you lack the confidence to do so or when you are terrified of being rejected.

Sometimes, a child with ADHD's mind is so busy that trying to make friends can seem like an unnecessary extra task. If a child with ADHD is content with being on their own, they are unlikely to make any effort to find friends or reciprocate when children try to initiate friendships with them.

Furthermore, remember that children with ADHD tend to interrupt and speak before thinking. It can be difficult to maintain friendships when others perceive you as rude. Interrupting others and saying things seemingly without a filter can drive people away.

Does ADHD disrupt the social relationships of those afflicted? Yes.

Emotions

ADHD affects the emotions of those afflicted. It's not uncommon for children with ADHD to develop other mental disorders like anxiety and depression. ADHD often brings along feelings of

- confusion
- loneliness
- disconnection
- not being in control
- being lost
- frustration
- overwhelm
- restlessness

Those with ADHD have a difficult time managing their emotions. A mild inconvenience not only irritates but absolutely infuriates those with ADHD. If something is exciting, it is the single *most important* thing in the world!

However, the direct impact of ADHD on one's emotions does not paint the full picture. I believe that the impact that ADHD has on each of the areas of life discussed above also affects our emotions:

- **Cognition:** Having a difficult time with impulsivity, inattentiveness, and hyperactivity can introduce a lot of distress and anxiety into the lives of those afflicted. Often, hyperactivity can cause mental exhaustion, impulsivity can cause difficult consequences, and inattentiveness can lead to big mistakes needing to be corrected.
- **Behavior:** Imagine constantly being reprimanded for behavior you have no control over. Imagine the feeling of betrayal from your body when you know you shouldn't be doing something but are doing it anyway. Imagine the feeling of worthlessness when you know you should be doing something but you just can't.
- **Work:** Struggling at work can cause major distress and anxiety in terms of maintaining a

job and continuing to make a living. Knowing you have these difficulties and trying to find a job in which you can excel can feel impossible. Ultimately, many people with ADHD are forced into work environments where they cannot excel, are not passionate, and simply work for the sake of making ends meet.
- **School:** Children with ADHD are so often categorized as "lazy" and "naughty." Imagine being in an environment where you are always belittled and thought of as "stupid" or "lazy" when, in actual fact, you are trying your best; you feel like you are trying harder than anyone around you and are never achieving the same results. Imagine throwing so much physical and mental effort into something, only to achieve the bare minimum and be told that you "aren't trying hard enough" or you "don't care enough."
- **Social Relationship:** Feelings of loneliness and being misunderstood can make those with ADHD feel extremely isolated. Having ADHD can feel like your mind is working at a frequency that no other person can hear or comprehend. It can feel like you are trapped in a place where you have no control over yourself. You can easily feel like a prisoner in your own body.

ADHD can, and does, have extreme effects on the emotions of those afflicted.

So, when you break it down, ADHD is absolutely a disorder and should be recognized as such. ADHD can, and does, inhibit and disrupt the lives of those with the condition. And, just as with any other disorder, those with it deserve help and support to find ways to not only cope but also achieve and excel despite their condition.

In Spite of That

As with all big, scary storm clouds, there is a silver lining to ADHD as well. In fact, there are many. ADHD is definitely a challenge, but it also offers those who have it many wonderful abilities and characteristics that are invaluable.

Wonderful strengths that come along with ADHD include the following:

- creativity and ability to think out of the box, offering unique and new perspectives to all sorts of situations
- incredible resilience that has built up through years of having to find solutions to the unique challenges they face

- great empathy and compassion for others, as they know first-hand how it feels to struggle constantly
- strength and perseverance

It is simply impossible for anyone without ADHD to have an exact understanding of what is happening inside the brain of someone with ADHD. Hell, even those with ADHD themselves often can't explain precisely what it feels like to live with a mind that operates on a rhythm not understood and often not accepted in this world. Yet, we have to try to understand. We have to learn as much as we can to care for our loved ones who are facing the challenges caused by the many obstacles they have in their way.

3

THE NEUROSCIENCE OF ADHD

I prefer to distinguish ADD as attention abundance disorder. Everything is just so interesting, remarkably at the same time.

— FRANK COPPOLA

Asking parents to have the ability to fully *understand* the way their child's ADHD mind works is asking a lot. Just as folk with ADHD cannot possibly fathom the mind of a neurotypical, a neurotypical simply cannot understand the mind of someone with ADHD.

Even though ADHD was "discovered" over 100 years ago, it is still a hugely misunderstood disorder (Holland, 2021). Only with recent technology have we been able to study ADHD through MRI scans and neuroimaging, and only recently has ADHD been recognized in adults as well as children.

The understanding of ADHD has greatly improved over the years. However, there is still so much more to unpack. To start understanding ADHD, perhaps we must begin with the scientific facts.

CAUSES OF ADHD

So, is ADHD a condition with which random people are born? Does fate arbitrarily pick and choose who will or won't have ADHD? Of course not. While the causes of ADHD are not yet fully understood, there are several different strong contributing factors that have been unearthed.

Because ADHD tends to run in families, researchers have reason to believe that genetics may be one possible cause of ADHD. It has been found that those with ADHD are likely to pass the condition down to their children. In fact, many parents are diagnosed with ADHD around the same time that their child is; as they watch their children be diagnosed, they end up identifying similar symptoms in themselves, as well.

This is where I find myself and my mother. In my case, my mother raised me, and though we considered our challenges exhausting, we never even pondered the idea that we might both have ADHD until much later in life. Years later, I once had someone ask me if I blame my parents for having ADHD, and I thought what a *ridiculous* thing to ask. How can you ever hold someone accountable for something they knew nothing about? Now that we are much better informed about our reality, both being diagnosed with ADHD is actually a point that has made our relationship stronger than before. ADHD became a shared interest or burden—depending on how you want to look at it, of course.

Because of this genetic inheritance, children with ADHD often have siblings with the condition as well. This goes to show that it is very likely that family genetics play a significant role in whether or not one has ADHD. However, it is also believed that ADHD cannot be chalked up to a single genetic discrepancy.

Another factor in the development of ADHD is the natural structure and anatomy of the brain. While studying this condition, researchers have identified a number of differences in the brain of those with ADHD compared to neurotypical brains. Often, certain areas are larger in ADHD brains while others are smaller than the neurotypical norm. The areas responsible for attention, activity levels, impulse control, and memory have lower activity levels in the brains of those with ADHD. There are even studies to suggest that those with ADHD may have issues with the level of neurotransmitters in the brain.

But the brain's natural physiological structure is not all that researchers have considered. They have also considered how alterations to that structure can introduce chemical imbalances or developmental issues. Two things are believed to have the potential to cause the types of alterations in the brain that may lead to ADHD: Firstly, physical trauma to the head. Secondly, childhood trauma. Trauma is known to disturb and alter the structure of the brain physically. These alterations can put a child at risk for developing ADHD or cause them to exhibit symptoms that mimic ADHD.

Childhood trauma refers to when someone experiences traumatic stress before the age of 18 years old. Traumatic stress may refer to experiences such as

- abuse—psychological, physical, or sexual
- emotional neglect
- physical neglect

- exposure to: substance abuse, mental illnesses, divorce, domestic violence, or incarceration

The key to understanding how trauma can induce ADHD symptoms is something called *toxic stress*. Toxic stress is the outcome of the body's stress management system being in "active mode" for a prolonged period of time, as it would be when experiencing childhood trauma.

When the body comes into contact with a stressor, it releases adrenaline and cortisol, the stress hormone. Adrenaline is what triggers your fight-or-flight response, while cortisol helps to prepare the body's energy stores and temporarily enhances memory.

For a "normal" stressor, this hormonal response will only last a few moments before the body calms down. However, in cases of traumatic experiences, this reaction from the body can be greatly extended, often coming in peaks and valleys. This is because being around people or environments associated with trauma can trigger a reaction in the body akin to if the trauma were occurring again. This prolonged stress response can result in toxic stress, and this is what can cause alterations in the brain, which may lead to ADHD or ADHD-like symptoms.

Though the brain is the main aspect affected by ADHD, it is not the only factor contributing to its development. Researchers are also looking into environmental factors relating to ADHD. They suggest that a fast-paced way of life may be to blame for ADHD, or at least for the level at which people with this neurotype find it debilitating. Children are exposed to rapid lifestyles and yet must then adjust to a classroom's slower pace. They are exposed to action-packed gaming and media that improve their speed of processing information but this influx of constant stimuli can introduce or exacerbate attention problems as children grow up constantly seeking the next source of entertainment.

But, just as it is important to talk about things that may cause ADHD, it is also important to eliminate the things that do *not* cause ADHD. There is no evidence to support any suggestion that food additives, allergies, immunizations, or eating too much sugar cause ADHD.

THE ADHD BRAIN VERSUS A NEUROTYPICAL BRAIN

We have mentioned how ADHD can affect the physical structure of the brain. But what do these structural differences mean for those living with ADHD? In the ADHD brain, there is an imbalance in the structural and functional connectivity of the brain. This means that, when faced with a task that must be done, certain areas of the brain become hyperactive while others become hypo(under)-active. This ultimately causes the brain to struggle with meeting the cognitive demands of the task.

Executive functions are the area of brain activity suffering the most significant impact. There are several ways how this impacts the life of your ADHD child. Dysregulation of this specific type of brain activity—known as *executive dysfunction*—leads to an inability to hold attention, concentrate, and focus for extended periods, causing difficulty in memorizing and recalling information. A person with executive dysfunction may struggle with decision-making and planning, which will impact the ability to engage self-control and motivation. As self-control is challenged, social skills are often consequently impaired and so is the ability to regulate emotions and reactions. As regulation is impacted, your ADHD child becomes impulsive and hyperactive.

As people grow, they usually slowly develop the executive functions that prevent this pattern of behavior. While neurotypical people often start this process at two years old and have their executive functions fully developed by the age of 30, people with ADHD are often 30–40% delayed in this development (Rodden,

2022). Yet, even with this delayed development, people with ADHD are expected to behave and respond in an age-appropriate manner.

So, how might one recognize the signs of executive dysfunction? A person's executive function is established based on the strength of these seven skills:

- self-awareness: being able to direct your own attention inward and reflect on your emotions, thoughts, and behaviors
- self-restraint: being able to inhibit yourself and avoid the temptation to follow strong but unhelpful urges
- non-verbal working memory: how well you can retain visual imagery in your mind—usually information having to do with sight, smell, taste, and touch
- verbal working memory: your inner monologue and ability to recall linguistic information
- emotional self-regulation: being able to influence your own emotional state using the four skills mentioned previously
- self-motivation: being able to prompt yourself into action when there is no external motivator or consequences

- planning and problem-solving: being able to come up with unique solutions and ideas

These executive functions are largely impacted by the fact that there is also a significant difference in how the neurotransmitters of the brain function in people with ADHD versus in neurotypical brains. The two main neurotransmitters associated with ADHD are dopamine and noradrenaline. In those with ADHD, there is dysregulation in the dopamine system. In other words, the brain is either lacking dopamine, lacking the necessary receptors for dopamine, or is using dopamine inefficiently.

Unfortunately, many of our executive functions are associated with dopamine, as dopamine is the "feel good" hormone that rewards you with a sense of pleasure when you have completed a task. The memory of this sense of pleasure acts as a motivation to continue doing something, to do something again, or to do something different to receive that sense of pleasure once more. At least, that's how it works in the neurotypical brain.

For those with ADHD, this is not the case. This release of dopamine often doesn't come, and as a result, there is no reward for completing a task, nor is there any motivation for doing the next. Contrastingly, sometimes the dopamine response is triggered too early in those with ADHD, meaning that we gain as much internal satisfaction from planning how to do something as a neurotypical person would from actually completing that task. This means that people with ADHD often schedule themselves into paralysis, anticipating that they will be more effective if they have a game plan going into a big project but then having no further motivation to continue once the plan is formed. Because the brain is designed to seek out behaviors that will release this dopamine, people will naturally continue to do the things that release dopamine and make them happy. Those with ADHD have to work twice as hard to receive that dose of dopamine, and often they will find it in other places, such as playing video games, eating junk food, partaking in a hobby, etc.

Dr. Kalley Spina Horan also highlights the following notable differences in the brain of someone with ADHD (2021):

- lower volume in the *caudate nucleus*, which is associated with motivation and goal-directed behavior
- lower volume in the *putamen*, associated with learning and motor control, as well as speech articulation

- a smaller *nucleus accumbens*, associated with emotional regulation, motivated behavior, and reward information
- a smaller *amygdala*, which is associated with experiencing emotions, detecting threats, and responding accordingly
- a smaller *cerebellum*, which is associated with the coordination of motor movements; this includes balance, posture, the way you walk, muscle tone, and voluntary muscle movement
- slower development of the *prefrontal cortex*, which is responsible for self-awareness, self-regulation, insight, decision-making, judgment, and behavior
- a larger *hippocampus*, which is associated with long-term memory and working memory

It is due to these many changes in the brain that ADHD is so often paired with another type of mental disorder. One of the most common disorders to be paired with ADHD is anxiety. The inability to regulate their emotions can lead to a low tolerance for frustration, conflict, or other stressors. Children with ADHD often respond to a difficult task or conflict with anger and fear, becoming emotionally and physically upset. Unfortunately, this is often misinterpreted as bad behavior.

Another noticeable physical difference between the ADHD brain and a neurotypical brain is that the development of the cortex thickness of the ADHD brain is roughly three years slower than that of a neurotypical brain. While these kids are managing with executive functions on the same level as someone three years their junior, we expect them to remain on par with others their age. The added pressure the ADHD child has to face is often simply because too many parents are not well-informed on the differences between the neurotypical and ADHD brain.

So, what are you to do when you suspect your child may be struggling beyond the point of your parental reach? Getting a positive diagnosis would be key to ensuring your child can get optimal treatment and start to develop coping mechanisms to make life a little more pleasant for themself and you.

4

DIAGNOSING ADHD AND TREATMENT OPTIONS

Once you eliminate the impossible, whatever remains, no matter how improbable, must be the truth.

— SIR ARTHUR CONAN DOYLE

You may have picked up this book because your child's teacher mentioned ADHD during that parent-teacher conference last week. Perhaps, you have read through the symptoms of ADHD and have recognized those behaviors in your child. You may be dead sure of the fact that your child is most *definitely* struggling with ADHD.

Or you may be on the other side of the spectrum. Perhaps, your child has been "acting up," and you just can't tell what's happening with them. You may have "tried everything" to get them back on track, to no avail. Perhaps, you have an inkling that something is causing this behavior, but you aren't sure what exactly that might be.

In which of these scenarios is a professional diagnosis necessary?

SHOULD I GET MY CHILD DIAGNOSED?

The answer is always, yes. If you ever suspect your child of having a mental or physical health issue, it is always best practice to go to a pediatrician or mental healthcare professional to receive a professional diagnosis. Why? From a parental viewpoint, there are several reasons why you should find a diagnosis as early on as possible. However, none of these will mean as much to your child as the impact of finding that confirmation that they are not just awkward or not fitting in. A child's world can be a very harsh and unforgiving place. At that age, the emotional maturity needed to not take the comments of peers to heart hasn't developed yet. Therefore, prior to diagnosis, your child only has themselves to blame for their behavior, but after a positive diagnosis, there is a valid explanation, taking the weight of guilt and uncertainty off their shoulders. Though I was only diagnosed in my adult life, I, too, felt that I could breathe a little deeper when I finally had an explanation for what I'd been going through. A diagnosis may not heal past scars, but it sure does wonders for self-esteem and make the future a little easier.

To Provide Effective Treatment

Because a professional diagnosis is the only surefire way to ensure your child receives the help, training, or medication, they require to survive and thrive in this life. Getting a proper diagnosis ensures that you, your family, and any friends or teachers are well-equipped with the proper information and understanding to provide your child with the necessary help and accommodations.

Alertness to Other Possible Concerns

When you are aware of the challenges your child is facing, you'll also be able to notice any other conditions much sooner as you are now alerted to the fact that they have ADHD and are likely going to face other concerns too. I am referring, here, to the increased likelihood of depression, anxiety, learning disabilities, and other previously discussed conditions. As parents, we want to do what is best for our children; when we know better, we can do better.

Ruling Out Traumatic Stress

While it is good to know what other conditions we need to look out for, a positive diagnosis will also rule out any other serious medical concerns that may require urgent attention and can cause similar symptoms. Here, I am specifically referring to traumatic stress. Traumatic stress and ADHD share several symptoms:

- finding it difficult to learn
- having trouble concentrating
- being disorganized
- hyperactivity
- restlessness
- trouble sleeping
- struggling to listen

While the two concerns share the above symptoms, they each demand intervention through their own specific treatment options. The approach to addressing ADHD and traumatic stress differs, and as they both demand urgent attention, it is vital to get a professional diagnosis for clarity regarding the treatment option.

Rule Out Possible Medical Conditions

Some serious medical concerns can cause symptoms very similar to those of ADHD. These include medical conditions like epilepsy, strokes, and rapid brain seizures. Understandably, these medical conditions can have a dire impact on your child's life if they aren't addressed with the correct treatment. Conversely, early detection and proper treatment can avoid serious consequences.

I believe that the uncertainty linked to whether something is wrong often drives our stress levels beyond what can possibly be healthy. Once we know the answers, the puzzle pieces fit, and we can start to make progress. The first state of being is entirely unproductive and not proactive in relieving your or your child's stress or condition. The second option—getting a professional diagnosis—is what makes the difference in your life and that of your child. Then, you can begin to move forward and overcome the challenge ahead.

GETTING A PROPER DIAGNOSIS

Great, now you know getting a proper, professional diagnosis is a valuable step in the journey. You understand that it is vital to proceed to gain the insights of a professional into your child's behavior, but as you are no medical expert yourself, how do you know if the diagnosis you've received was proper and accurate? Your child may have been misdiagnosed. These things happen. So, naturally, your own fears kick in: Should you get a second or maybe a third opinion, too?

Understanding what a proper diagnosis looks like may put your mind at ease. Once again, grasping the power that knowledge adds makes life as the parent of an ADHD child a little easier. It gives you the confidence of *knowing*, even when all other matters in your life seem to rob you of your confidence in your ability to be a great parent.

To have a proper diagnosis, your medical professional has to use the guidelines for a positive ADHD diagnosis as stipulated by the *American Psychiatric Association*'s *Diagnostic and Statistical Manual, Fifth Edition* (DSM-5).

If your child is younger than 16, they will need to portray six of the following symptoms to ensure a positive diagnosis, and if they are 17 or older, they would need to test positive on five symptoms. The CDC shares the following as the symptoms stipulated in the DSM-5 linked to inattention (*Symptoms and diagnosis of ADHD*, 2022):

- failing to pay attention and making careless mistakes

- struggling to hold their attention during tasks and activities
- an inability to follow instructions
- having challenges in organizing duties and responsibilities
- disliking and even avoiding tasks demanding prolonged mental focus
- losing and misplacing their possessions often
- getting distracted easily
- being very forgetful

The symptoms linked to hyperactivity are

- fidgeting and tapping of hands or feet or squirming in seats
- getting up from their seat at inappropriate times
- not being able to play quietly
- excessive talking
- talking out of their turn
- an inability to wait for their turn to come
- always being active and running around
- interrupting others or intruding on them

Yet, a positive diagnosis would also require the following additional requirements to be met:

- Several symptoms must have been present in your child's behavior before they turned 12.
- Your child must show concerning behavior in at least two different settings, meaning at school and home, at home and when visiting friends, or with friends and at school.
- It must be clear that your child's behavior is restricting their growth as it keeps them from functioning at their best.
- Then, also, there must be no other way to explain the symptoms your child is portraying. Through elimination, the medical professional must be able to dismiss all other possible causes for the behavior, leaving only ADHD as the answer.

Knowing the criteria for a positive diagnosis makes it easier for you—as the parent and not a mental health expert—to pose informed questions to your doctor to gain more information regarding your child's diagnosis.

TYPES OF POSITIVE DIAGNOSIS

How would they present this information to you? Your child can have one of three different types of positive diagnosis to confirm ADHD:

- **Predominantly inattentive** presentation means your child tested positive for inattention but not hyperactivity-impulsivity.
- **Predominantly hyperactive-impulsive** presentation refers to a positive diagnosis of hyperactivity-impulsivity but not inattention.
- **Combined** presentation means your child shows enough symptoms to confirm a positive diagnosis for inattention and hyperactivity-impulsivity.

All three would only be diagnosed following confirmation that sufficient symptoms were present for the past six months before the diagnosis.

Understanding what type of presentation your child has helps to narrow down the specific treatment options to help them specifically.

So, as you can see, there is a relatively comprehensive list of required symptoms needed to confirm that your child has ADHD. The next burning question you may have is linked to who you should trust to take care of this testing. It is often the case that many people might have an opinion about your child, and sometimes these voices can echo in your head. While many might share their ideas, you can only be sure of the actual diagnosis when you schedule an appointment with a properly qualified specialist.

Only licensed mental health practitioners and physicians have the knowledge and expertise to offer you a positive diagnosis. Under the umbrella term of a physician, you'll find physicians like your family doctor, psychiatrists, psychologists, neurologists, or any other qualified medical doctor. Thus, you can reach out to your family doctor, a professional who most likely knows your child much better and have a deeper understanding of your family dynamics, to make such a diagnosis or referral to the appropriate specialist.

ADHD TREATMENT OPTIONS

Once your child has received a positive diagnosis, you finally know exactly why your child is behaving the way they are. This is a significant moment in your relationship, and you may very well experience a bunch of emotions. While you may feel sympathy for your child, you may not understand the complete picture of your little one's future. You know they face challenges other children don't have to deal with. But you are also glad to have an answer; knowing why your child is acting out, often in trouble, always late, and underperforming can be liberating to a certain degree. Naturally, you may also feel relieved—even though you may not express this verbally as you are scared that it sounds selfish—glad that it is not your parenting skills that failed your child. It is good to know that you are not to blame for the challenges your child and the entire family are facing. The last thing any great parent wants is for their faults or inadequacies to be the cause of their child's challenges.

Then, there is also that sense of being overwhelmed. The four letters, A-D-H-D, demand a significant reshuffle in your lives, routines, and approach to everything related to your child and the rest of your family. How do you move forward from this point? Immediately, you may feel the bitter pangs of anxiety creep up again. You are torn between seeking certainty in your approach to managing your child's symptoms and not making a hasty decision. Added to this mixture of emotions is your exhausted mind and body, for while all the tension of seeking a diagnosis has been weighing on you, little Tommy, Sarah, Mandy, or Keith hasn't stopped their behavior. A positive diagnosis hasn't changed anything in how they behave. Nothing, zilch, nada has improved simply because you have a confirmation on paper. ADHD is not like a cold or the flu; it's not like once your doctor confirms what is wrong, you get a prescription, pop your meds, and viola! Within a few days, it is all over. No, no, no. ADHD is a lifelong journey; you're only taking the first steps now.

Knowing what treatment options there are will clarify your confusion, but before going any further, understand that there is not one treatment option that will transform your child's behavior. The best results are usually the outcome of applying several different methods to work together, as ADHD children do the best when their behavior is addressed with a holistic approach.

Therapy

Several different therapy options will be beneficial. It will help if you are determined—with the help of your child's teachers and the professionals who are part of your child's support network—to decide which therapy works the best. You will also need to consider your budget, as it is an unfortunate reality that not every parent can afford the best and most comprehensive therapeutic approach to address their family's challenges due to ADHD.

The list of helpful therapy options usually includes

- Behavioral Therapy and Social Skills Training: Both these types of therapy can help your child learn better coping skills when exposed to large crowds, in social settings, and in other public places. Experts will work with your child to teach them skills to manage themselves more effectively. They will practice these changes to ensure that they become your child's go-to behavior choices.

- Family therapy: There are so many dynamics that come to play when one child is diagnosed. This therapy can equip your entire family to cope better with your situation. It can help you to be a better parent to your ADHD child and their siblings, and it will help you to be a better partner to your spouse. If you are a single parent, the family therapist can assist with coping tools to address your situation, and the person whose help you seek can become vital support in the structure of your network.

Finding an Education Plan

Your child is not the first or only—and will surely not be the last—child with ADHD sitting in the classrooms at their school. Work with your child's teachers to create an education plan that will benefit your child. Once your child is diagnosed, they are no longer the naughty one or the one who is always acting out. If you've previously perceived frustration linked to your child's behavior from their teachers, you may very likely observe a shift in mindset on their side too. They are qualified professionals trained to work with children facing all challenges. However, if you are not getting the cooperation you need from your child's teachers and are not unfair in your demands, don't hesitate to explore other options. In the long run, it is better to cause a disruption early on by changing schools than to endure the stress of a lack of cooperation from teachers who ought to be your confidants but, in reality, are not.

Making Lifestyle Changes

Your child can reap many benefits from changing their diet, ensuring their minds and bodies get the nutrition they need, and including sufficient exercise in their daily routines. Addressing gut health is also essential, and we'll dig a little deeper into this soon.

Medication

Why do I mention medication last when it is so often assumed that the answer to ADHD is nestled in the correct medication? Simply because medication is not the answer to all your child's challenges. Yes, it will help, but you will most likely have to go through trials and errors to find the right prescription to support your child. Moreover, it is not the only answer. Medication alone will not bring you the outcome you are hoping for.

Nevertheless, it is worth being aware of the types of medicine licensed and prescribed to treat ADHD symptoms. Take note, I say *ADHD symptoms* and not ADHD. ADHD never heals. Your child can't "recover" from it, because your child isn't broken by it. They are merely struggling with certain aspects of their being, and the medicine listed below can help them address and manage these symptoms much better to enjoy greater satisfaction and success in life (NHS, 2021b):

- methylphenidate
- lisdexamfetamine
- dexamfetamine
- atomoxetine
- guanfacine

Each of these hard-to-pronounce names has a list of benefits and side effects. You must work with your physician to find the right balance and solutions to best support your child. This process can take a while as not all of these medications show instant results. Unless otherwise stated, these options are safe for children older than 5 and mostly work on brain areas responsible for behavior and attention management.

Methylphenidate

This is a stimulant and the most common choice to address ADHD symptoms. It can be taken in smaller doses during the day, offering a fast-release, or one slow-release tablet in the morning.

What are the side effects you need to be alerted of?

- stomach pain
- headaches
- a minor increase in blood pressure and, as a result thereof, heart rate
- weight loss due to a poor appetite
- insomnia
- an increase in depression and anxiety symptoms
- being more tense and aggressive

Lisdexamfetamine

If the previous option brings no signs of improvement, doctors often try lisdexamfetamine next. This is available in capsule format and requires taking only one pill daily.

The side effects are similar to those of methylphenidate, with only a few variations:

- headaches
- increased aggression
- decreased appetite resulting in weight loss
- diarrhea

- nausea and vomiting
- dizziness
- drowsiness

Dexamfetamine

Dosages of this pharmaceutical option are taken 2–4 times per day in a table form, but you can also ask for an oral solution, as not all kids are great with taking tablets and capsules.

Here too, there is no escape from possible side effects:

- diarrhea
- nausea and vomiting
- headaches
- dizziness
- easily agitated and increased aggression
- mood swings
- decreased appetite

Atomoxetine

This option differs from all other possible solutions because it is a noradrenaline reuptake inhibitor (SNRI). In lay terms, it increases the uptake of the hormone noradrenaline in the brain. Noradrenaline can pass through the cells and improve concentration, improving how behavior is managed. It is a safe option for anyone older than five but is usually not the first option to prescribe for ADHD.

If this option is prescribed, your child will have to take a capsule once or twice per day, and the following side effects may occur:

- a slight increase in blood pressure and heart rate
- sleep troubles
- headaches
- stomach aches
- nausea and vomiting
- dizziness
- increase irritability

In some instances, this prescription causes several other more severe side effects, including increased suicidal thoughts. Therefore, when your child is prescribed atomoxetine, be sure to discuss all possible side effects with your doctor, learning exactly what signs you need to look out for.

Guanfacine

This active ingredient lowers blood pressure and increases attention. Although never prescribed for adults, it is a safe option for children older than five and teenagers. Your kid would have to take a table once a day.

Guanfacine has fewer side effects:

- dry mouth
- abdominal pain
- headaches
- fatigue

I know these side effects can seem overwhelming, and it sounds like you are giving your child poison rather than an aid to help them along. Remember that, by law, it is necessary to inform every patient of all possible side effects, but just because a particular prescription has shown certain side effects in the past for other people and was recorded as such doesn't mean your child will experience the same side effects. Just be alert of what can happen, so you can know what is going on and inform your doctor as needed.

POSITIVE PARENTING TIP

There is nobody better equipped than you to draft a treatment plan or strategy than you. You are the one who cares the most about your child's well-being, loves them, and whose life is affected the most, apart from their own.

You are familiar with the circumstances in your home, your financial and time restraints, the challenges you are facing, and the minor details of life as your child knows it.

While you will work with your medical professional to finalize the finer details of the plan, you can start drafting such a plan by consulting your child. *What will make your life easier?* A simple question that can have such a comprehensive answer. It is a question you may have to ask several times and in several ways to understand as best as you can what is going on in your child's mind.

Once you have clarity on your child's needs, you have a foundation to draft your plan. There is no set format for such a plan, as every child and family is unique. The benchmark for a successful plan would be one where the outcome is that your child's life and the aspects they enjoy improve. They should be able to better manage and organize their lives to obtain more effective results.

An effective structure to follow would be to set a timeline and indicate certain measurable objectives your child and you would like to achieve along the way. In the plan, you need to consider your child's personality, needs, family routines, and the extracurricular activities of all family members. *What does your child desire? What does your family desire?*

A specific point your plan can address is improved behavior, as it is a set objective on the timeline. A few goals, in this regard, might include your child's portrayed behavior improving and their undesired actions decreasing. Another can be to address self-awareness and help your child to become more aware of who they are, their identity, strengths and weaknesses, and how they can feel better about themselves.

Once completed, your treatment plan will become a guideline, supporting you in sustaining better physical health too.

5

STRENGTHEN THE BODY AND CALM THE BRAIN

Forgive your child and yourself nightly. You didn't ask to live with the effects of ADHD any more than did your child.

— MARTIN L. KUTSCHER

A healthier kid is a happier kid that is just a natural law. You know that it is not just in your home that this applies, as any parent, even those of neurotypical kids, will confirm that a healthy family is a happy family, making life far less stressful and exhausting for parents. Also, taking care of your own health is crucial. If you are not feeling your best, it will be much harder to stay calm, manage your emotions, and be able to deliver all that is expected of you, including supporting your child through their own concerns.

Good health doesn't only involve preventing colds and flu. Yes, it is horrible to be sick while your family still needs you, and the worst of all concerns is probably having to deal with a tummy bug or a home full of people suffering from this acute, inconvenient medical concern. But good health also refers to living a healthy lifestyle that will reduce stress, increase focus, and allow you to feel energetic, positive, and capable of taking on another day with love and courage.

If you are already managing a relatively healthy lifestyle, I want to congratulate you on doing exceptionally well. It is often our health that we would neglect first.

CULTIVATING A HEALTHY AND BALANCED LIFESTYLE FOR YOUR CHILD

A balanced and healthy lifestyle depends on several aspects, including exercising and getting the correct nutrition.

Exercise

Let's start by exploring what types of exercise will deliver the best benefits and why it is essential.

Your diary is full, and you are overburdened, I get all that. But simply taking a short, brisk walk will be enough to release the feel-good hormones in your brain, putting your mind and body in a much better space with minimal effort. Not to mention that this short time out—being on your own and doing something for you—will have a lasting positive impact, giving you just a little push to feel better, and I am all for embracing every little thing that can help us make it through the day. If you have someone who can keep an eye on your child, even if it is only for about half an hour, take it, thank them, and get out to have that walk. Trust me, it will leave you feeling better.

But let's move our focus to your child. You are likely already struggling to keep your kid just a little calmer. You get exhausted by just looking at them as they are so active. Do they even need more exercise? Yes!

The beauty of regular exercise is that it doesn't only improve the emotional and physical health of your child with ADHD, but it also helps to better manage their symptoms. Some other benefits to exercise are that it will help your child to focus better, feel less confused, and be more motivated. Exercise has many benefits similar to that of ADHD medication, without all the side effects. Never substitute medication with only exercise, but instead, see it as a supporting act in your complete treatment plan to reap the benefits.

The ideal "dose" of this complementary medication is around 30–40 minutes of exercise per day, 4–5 days a week. But if you can't see how you'll be able to devote so much time to ensuring your child is getting in the necessary exercise, start with whatever you have time for. Gradually, you can increase the time. We'd rather start small than do nothing at all.

You should aim for "moderate exercise." The exercise your child is doing should be strenuous enough that their heart rate goes up, they are sweating, and they must breathe faster. You can opt for many types of exercise: running, swimming laps, biking (if possible, in nature), and taking a brisk walk. Another fantastic exercise that kids often love and that will help them to learn better control over their emotions—training their mind and body to work as a team—is martial arts. See if there are any judo, karate, taekwondo, or jiu jitsu classes in your area. Reach out to the sensei, and chat with them about what you would like to achieve by bringing your child to them. Who knows, maybe this person can become another vital support structure in your network, helping make life a little easier for your child. Martial arts teaches children—neurodivergent and neurotypical, alike—how to improve their balance, timing, and fine motor skills, but it also increases their focus and concentration and teaches that there are consequences to their actions.

Other sports that are high up on the list of physical activities that have helpful ADHD benefits are dancing, rock climbing, yoga, and gymnastics, as all of these options demand more of your child than merely being active, needing them to take control over their actions and movements.

How can you keep your child hooked on exercise? As exercise is such an essential part of their treatment plan, you should give it the same level of importance as taking medicine regularly. It helps if your child is interested in the specific type of exercise they're undertaking. Maybe, switch between several types of activities to keep things new, exciting, and dopamine-inducing. It will also help if they make a friend in the group they are exercising with, as they then have an exercise buddy.

The best place to practice any form of exercise is outdoors. Nature has a wonderfully calming effect on the mind and body. So, the more often you can enable your child to get their fitness dose for the day in nature, the greater the benefits will be. Nature is, by design, a place where we get more fresh air, but it is also, by design, somewhere we can discharge negative energy. Here, you'll be surrounded by soothing natural elements, as there is less exposure to noise pollution, lots of calming green tones, and nature's sound. Nature is where we can go to break away from the rushed pace of life that is doing neither you nor your child any good.

When venturing into nature, try to regularly include natural environments offering great calming qualities. Nature does surround us, but not all natural settings are of the same quality. Thus, try to take that well-deserved break on the weekend and venture with your child into parks or go to a nearby lake. Identify natural break-away destinations where you can go to help your child relax to the max in a quality natural environment.

Eating

When your child has been on meds for a couple of weeks (or longer), quickly you notice that their appetite is almost non-existent. You can see how they lose weight, which is rightfully concerning. Now, I am telling you that your child should still eat—though you already know that—and that they should sustain a healthy diet, eating food that is good for them.

Remember that ADHD doesn't cause a loss of appetite or the weight loss that goes with it; the medication they need to take does that to them. Add to that the challenge that your child may also be sensorily sensitive and reject specific foods that smell, taste, or feel a certain way. Then, you may also be facing some other individual challenges unique to your child.

Scheduled Eating

Have you slipped into a routine of giving your child something to eat throughout the day, believing that the more you try to get them to eat, the higher the odds are in your favor that they'll eat something—*anything*? This is an entirely understandable act of desperation, but it won't benefit your child long term. Rather, set specific times for eating and snacking. Stick to these times, as this is a way to train the brain to feel hungry and gets your body in the routine of expecting food to come into the digestive system at set times.

When kids are grazing as they feel, their bodies never get used to building an appetite. Don't force your child to eat when it is time for eating, but rather, make it an opportunity for them to eat and limit the chances that fall outside this timeframe.

When you are already concerned about your child's weight loss, you may feel even more pressed to get them to eat something. Kids who can sustain an optimal weight for their age grow faster and stronger and can keep up with their developmental stages. Rather than increasing the number of times you would try to get them to eat, change the food you are offering during the eating windows. Certain healthy foods can help to increase weight gain, like

- pasta
- peanut butter
- nuts
- drumsticks
- deli meats
- milk
- yogurt
- canned and dried fruits
- potatoes
- sweet potatoes
- muffins
- bagels
- jellies and jams
- some cereals

You can also sneak more calories into their food by adding butter to their rice and pasta or trying to add sauces, olive oil, and cheese. Give them whole milk instead of skimmed milk, and add dips for their fruit.

Always read the labels of any new food product you are introducing into your child's diet as you have to be alert of colorants, preservatives, and flavorings manufacturers use in these foods. Some of these chemicals can have an adverse effect on your child.

Mood Foods

It will help to get familiar with mood foods—foods that naturally uplift the mood as their chemical composition is of such a manner that it makes it easier, physiologically, to feel good. These foods include fatty fish that are high in omega oils. You can opt for salmon or tuna. Sardines are also a great source of omega-3s, which are known to improve depression symptoms.

Dark chocolate is another option, as it contains just enough sugar and other compounds to make your brain feel good, and it also contains caffeine and other beneficial compounds to improve your mood. Also, try bananas, oats, berries, nuts, seeds, beans, lentils, and—one that kids, in general, don't like, but that is excellent—fermented foods. Usually, kids don't like the taste of fermented foods, and a lot of grown-ups don't like it either, but food like kefir, sauerkraut, and even live yogurt are fantastic foods to have as they improve the state of gut health which, counterinutitively, hugely impacts neurotransmitter availability.

Keep Them Hydrated

There is a general lack of understanding of how important it is to drink enough water affecting the lives of a great many people across the globe. Most people know that their bodies need water, but far fewer people realize that their brains need to remain hydrated too.

This is because water plays a vital role in the body. It aids in circulation, ensuring oxygen, hormones, nutrients, and energy are taken to where they are needed, and it helps the body get rid of toxins. The latter, of course, is of even greater importance when your child is on long-term medication, opening up the possibility of several side effects.

This is also why dehydration can cause anxiety symptoms. By ensuring your child drinks enough water, you reduce their chances of experiencing anxiety and depression symptoms, and you can lower their stress levels. Several studies have proven that when the body enters a state of dehydration, it becomes extra vulnerable to tension and depression. Another symptom caused by a lack of water consumption is increased confusion, another concern best avoided.

Gut Health

Gut health will always surface when we address mental and emotional challenges, as this part of the digestive system dramatically impacts our overall well-being.

Studies exploring children's gut health have taught us that as children grow older, the diversity of the microbes in the gut area diversifies. That means a baby will have a smaller number of different microbes than a child of six, for example. Similarly, a child of six will have far fewer different types of organisms in their gut than an adult. These studies also show that we were wrong to think that the greater the diversity of these organisms, the smaller the chance of getting ADHD. It is often the case that the gut of children with ADHD is far more mature than expected at their age (Cassidy-Brown, 2022).

There are a lot of factors that impact the pace at which your child's gut matures. For example, whether your child was fed breastmilk or formula will be the first aspect causing a difference in the state of their gut development. The same goes for babies who were born naturally versus those who were born through a C-section. This is because babies born naturally are exposed to bacteria in the birth canal. While no definitive studies confirm that either birthing option can impact your child's later chances of having ADHD, these are the first variables they may experience impacting their gut health and thus, if ADHD is present, the extent of certain elements of executive dysfunction.

However, as the choice of birthing option is most likely long behind you, a much better perspective on the matter would be to see if we can address the challenges we are facing by changing our current gut environment. Can probiotics make a difference in your child's symptoms? Some studies indicate that probiotics can improve neurodevelopment during the early childhood stages (Cassidy-Brown, 2022). Yet, even this research still needs more exploration to guide what you should add to your child's diet to improve ADHD symptoms through the gut. While probiotics are good for digestion and to improve overall gut health, it remains best to discuss any dietary adjustments with your child's doctor and get their take on the matter.

Otherwise, know that taking care of your gut and the other family members can only be beneficial. Researchers did confirm that sustained gut health is an essential contributing factor in supporting your immune system, preventing autoimmune and cardiovascular diseases, and minimizing endocrine and gastrointestinal disorders. Also, sustained gut health can reduce cancer and mental health concerns (Dix & Klein, 2022).

Sleep

Simply consider how short your fuse is when you are tired and how much more strain you have to put into biting your tongue when you are so drained. I think the most accurate reflection of a lack of sleep's impact on our mood can be seen in the behavior of a groggy toddler who hasn't had nap time. While it can be super challenging to get to sleep, we all know what it feels like to be so tired you can't manage your emotions, and yet, you just can't switch off your mind to take a break from thinking.

A lack of sleep for a couple of nights can be draining, but when you have chronic insomnia, your chances of developing various mental health concerns increase tremendously. The two most prominent concerns in this regard are depression and anxiety, and as we've already learned, simply due to having ADHD, your child is already more prone to both. Therefore, it would be beneficial for them to lose as little sleep as possible.

If this is a problem in your home, you can improve the state of matters by changing your child's habits surrounding their sleep time. A sleep routine will help. By going to bed and getting up at the same time every time, you train the brain to go into a calmer state at a specific time during the night.

Keep bedrooms for sleeping. Then, the mind will gradually start to associate the room with sleeping. Set a routine that indicates bedtime and keeps them away from any food that may contain chemicals that could keep them awake. Refraining from eating a couple of hours before bedtime will also help improve the quality of sleep, as will regular exercise.

ADHD Supplements

Sustaining optimal health includes giving their bodies what they need to do their best. So, we need to discuss supplements and what you can—and probably should—give your child as part of the holistic approach to improving their ADHD symptoms.

First, understand that supplements are more than medicine. Yes, they come in tablet or capsule form, or sometimes in syrup, so it can be easy to think they are just more chemicals you are pumping into the small body of your young child, but they aren't. A nutritional supplement contains the minerals and vitamins the body needs to perform optimally in a concentrated format. Let's put it this way, when will you be the most effective in ensuring your child gets what their body needs? In this example, omega-3 is what your child needs. Are you going to be able to get them to eat enough oily fish to be sure that they get all the omegas they need if they are already a picky eater with a suppressed appetite, or will you perform better if you only have to get them to take one more capsule, supplying the body with all the omega-3 it needs to sustain optimal brain health? When looking at supplements from this perspective, they can be a saving grace for the concerned parent.

What supplements will benefit your child?

- **Omega-3:** We can't discuss brain health without mentioning omega-3, as it is a vital building block of the brain's structure. Omega-3 plays a crucial role in cell signaling, improving communication between the brain and various body parts. So, omega-3 should definitely be on your list of daily supplements, but not just any omega-3. As with so much else in life, the cheaper the option, the poorer its quality, and you need to have a specific omega-3 combination to offer optimal support in this regard. Scan the labels of the omega-3 options you are considering to see if they contain EPA and DHA. The amount of EPA should be one-and-half times the DHA. Children can take 1,000mg of omega-3 daily, and teenagers can take 2,000 mg. As your child approaches adolescence, you can gradually increase their intake.

- **Zinc:** Studies have indicated that regular use of a zinc supplement can reduce the dosage of stimulants required by as much as 40% in ADHD cases (Newmark, 2022). It is possible to determine how significant your child's zinc deficiency is by having their blood tested, but without blood tests, you can safely give them 20–25 mg of zinc daily.
- **Vitamin D:** While many kids in the US already struggle with low vitamin D levels, these levels are even lower in children with ADHD. The importance of vitamin D even comes into play in infancy as scientists have found that the babies of mothers who had a vitamin D deficiency during their pregnancy are more likely to have ADHD. While no studies indicate that vitamin D supplements will improve the symptoms, it is essential to address the fact that they are already facing a deficiency that may be causing fatigue, depression, joint pain, or other concerning symptoms.
- **Iron:** This mineral is vital to ensure proper brain function, and we have scientific proof that iron supplements can improve ADHD

symptoms (Newmark, 2022). Before starting with any daily doses, first, have your child's blood tested to determine how significant any deficiency is to ensure you give them an optimal dosage. Too much iron or iron supplements of poor quality can cause constipation and stomach aches. Therefore, instead, get the necessary information first.

- **Magnesium:** This mineral contributes by calming a hyperactive child. It becomes beneficial in easing through those moments when the meds have worn off and it is not yet time for the following doses of medication. The suggested dosage would be 100–300 mg twice a day. There are three options: magnesium citrate, glycinate, or chelate. But do note that citrate can cause a runny tummy.
- **Vitamin C**: Vitamin C is well-known to help the body fight colds, but it also plays an essential role in producing dopamine and other neurotransmitters that help to manage their moods much better.
- **Melatonin:** Melatonin can help to combat sleep challenges, as it is known to help children with ADHD sleep much better.
- **Probiotics:** As mentioned, these can improve your child's gut health, but please discuss this

with your doctor first. As there are different types of probiotics, your medical expert will be able to advise you which to give your child and how much they recommend should be taken.

Herbal Supplements

- **Ginkgo Biloba**: has been used for ages for various purposes, but studies show that it can improve concentration in children with ADHD (Newmark, 2022).
- **Brahmi:** improves restlessness and can better attention span and self-control.
- **Green oats:** made of unripe oats, a known supplement to help with stress and anxiety, as their natural properties calm the nerves.
- **Ginseng:** also vital in improving concentration, relieves anxiety, and can help your child's social functioning skills.
- **Pine bark extract:** minimizes hyperactivity and, therefore, also helps to better attention span and concentration.

So, there is a lot that you can do that will improve your child's symptoms along with the medication they are taking. Managing ADHD well does require a comprehensive approach that will include many aspects of nutrition, rest, and activity. What you shouldn't do is go to stock up on every single item listed here. Rather, discuss nutrition and supplements with your medical practitioner who is familiar with your child's symptoms, and work with them to find the perfect balance of supplements to bring your child's overall health into an optimal state.

I also need you to remember that "if a little of something is good, then more of it should be better" is *not* the approach you should take when it comes to supplements. Also, not every child will enjoy the same benefits from a specific supplement. There are just too many variables that impact the outcome you'll see from taking any supplement. Yet, through continuous testing, you'll be able to find the success recipe for your child, defining the medication, supplements and herbs, food, and amount of exercise and sleep they need. Trial and error are, unfortunately, the only way to success.

Story Time

We should never underestimate food's important role in improving and sustaining our health. When we shift our mindset from considering food merely as something that fills our bellies and stills the hunger pains to something that feeds our bodies and cares for their every need, an entirely new world of healing opens up.

This is when you'll perceive food as medicine; when you do, the need for medication decreases.

When we consider food to be something intended to provide the body with nutrition, it becomes easier to recognize that our bodies need more of certain foods while other food is not suitable for our bodies. It may be that your child's body simply isn't a great fit for certain foods, even if they are nutritious. Alice's story is one of the many success stories that took place once she changed her approach toward what she ate.

Long before Alice was diagnosed with ADHD, her body had already shown that it didn't do well when digesting gluten or dairy. However, it was only once her symptoms after eating either became worse that her mother changed her diet, and she was diagnosed with lactose and gluten intolerance.

About two years later, her ADHD diagnosis followed. Yet, while already cutting wheat and dairy products, she still never felt great and would often struggle with such severe acid reflux that it would leave her feeling congested. Coupled with the fact that stomach acid can also increase your heart rate, she would often feel anxious after eating.

Medication for treating her acid problem became her daily staple. When Alice turned 16, she became fed up with all the meds she had to take, and she convinced her mother to take her to a nutritionist. He made several suggestions, and Alice followed his advice and cut even more food from her regular diet. While she had far more limited food options, she felt much better and no longer needed medicine to control her acid reflux. Gradually, her health improved, and she felt better—physically and mentally—than ever before. Eventually, she and her parents addressed her ADHD medication and the required doses with her doctor. The team worked together and gradually reduced the amount of medication Alice needed.

Today, Alice is almost 20, and it has been years since she has had to use any acid reflux medication. She is feeling great and is sustaining herself with much lower doses of ADHD meds, simply because she changed the way she was eating.

Drafting an eating plan is only one part of a much larger plan you will need to help your child to become the best version of themselves. But by setting an example and guiding them on how to follow this nutritional schedule, they will also learn valuable skills for organizing their lives as a whole. This guidance will include how they prioritize their responsibilities, plan activities, and, very importantly, manage their emotions.

6

MANAGING EMOTIONS

Be patient with me. Understand why I do the things I do. Don't yell at me. Believe me, I don't want to have ADHD.

— JOANNE E. RICHARDSON

You woke up tired like most other mornings. The amount of sleep you can get is just not enough to provide your body with the rest it needs. This is nothing new to you, nor are the many arguments you'll need to have to get your child ready for school. It is your daily routine, and you are used to facing all these challenges. Take note, I said I *used to* but not *comfortable with*. Sometimes, you wish your life was easier, your child the perfect student, homework done, excited to go to school. Nonetheless, these are the good days. There are days when your child can truly rock the fragile boat keeping you safe and sane. On these days, they are emotional. The slightest deviation from the routine they are used to can cause a massive emotional outburst. For example, the emotional meltdown Sally experienced when one of her shoes was missing this morning, or the way little Ben chucks all his pencils off the table just because one broke off in the sharpener. Why? Oh, why?

The answer can be pretty straightforward or highly complex: It all depends on whether you want to know the reason to ease your mind or are actually looking for a solution to resolve this concern. The latter is the more complex version. The simple answer is that your child just can't manage their emotions with ease. They are physically incapable of managing their feelings as a neurotypical child would. Even though this may be something you are already familiar with, why is it the case, and what can you do to ease their life and yours?

BECOMING EMOTIONALLY INTELLIGENT

As the parent of a child with ADHD, being emotionally intelligent will make your life and your responsibility towards your child, other family members, and yourself much easier. Emotional intelligence refers to your ability to effectively manage the feelings you are experiencing and those of others (*6 Steps to improve your emotional intelligence*, 2018).

Emotional intelligence consists of portraying three skills effectively. It demands that you have emotional awareness allowing you to witness the emotions others are experiencing and to identify what they are feeling and your feelings. It also entails using emotions effectively to overcome obstacles and achieve desired outcomes. The last aspect of emotional intelligence is managing your feelings and learning how to calm others down or lift the mood of someone sad or depressed.

When there is a lack of emotional intelligence, the consequences are often the expression of all feelings in the form of aggression, regardless of what actual feelings are heightened at that moment. Just because you are an adult, or even a parent, doesn't mean that you are naturally emotionally intelligent. Vast numbers of people don't even ponder the idea of emotional intelligence to determine whether they are equipped in this way.

As the parent in this relationship, being emotionally intelligent and taking the necessary steps to become better at identifying, expressing, and managing your own and others' emotions can be one of the most effective ways to equip yourself for the journey ahead. It can also be a way to model the behavior you want your child to adopt.

But where do you start? Before making any progress, you need to identify your shortcomings. How well are you able to identify your emotions and those of others? How often do you attend to your feelings? Questions such as these will build your self-awareness and equip you to further increase your emotional intelligence.

The next step in becoming more emotionally intelligent is to take action steps that allow you to portray more emotional intelligence. Initially, being more emotionally competent will be a forced process. You will have to consciously work at competence, but this is already better than being incompetent in the skills that can help your child and not even being aware of it.

Luckily, as with every other habit or skill, the more you do it, the easier it becomes. Recall all those stressful and exhausting moments when you learned to drive a car or ride a bicycle. It was hard, and if you are in any way like me, you may have thought several times that you'll never be able to get it right. There are just so many things you need to consider all at once. The task demanded that you concentrate all the time, as you had to focus on every aspect of what you were doing to ensure you were managing it correctly. Now, that skill has become a part of your life that you no longer even think about, looking in your mirrors when changing lanes or signaling at an intersection. No, it just happens, and the same can soon occur when you practice the skills I will be sharing with you. But before we get to that, I want us to explore why your child with ADHD struggles so much with managing their emotions. Here too, there are several good reasons for this concern, and none of these reasons are the unwillingness or stubbornness you might sometimes have the urge to blamer.

ADHD AND THE BRAIN CONNECTIONS

Your ADHD child experiences emotions much stronger than any neurotypical child. These kids struggle especially with frustration, impatience, and excitability. This is why the missing shoe or the broken pencil point turns into such a volatile moment. One emotion is enough to rob your child of focus and sweep them off into a downward spiral of stress and anxiety, an emotional whirlwind pulling your entire family into a tizz.

Thankfully, we know the scientific reason why this is typical behavior: The brain connections of the ADHD child are just different. They don't work as effectively as in a neurotypical brain, causing the brain to be flooded by emotions rather than opting for logical thinking.

Moreover, the ADHD child operates on instant gratification. You can tell your youngest to wait before opening the Christmas gifts until everyone is present, and they'll understand and follow your instructions. Your ADHD child will simply start ripping open parcels without delay, even at times opening packets that don't have their name on them, causing much unhappiness during this supposedly joyous and exciting occasion.

Additionally, working memory reduces the energy available to fuel an emotional response by using it to self-regulate. As the working memory of your ADHD child is not in an optimal state, they have more emotional energy that needs an escape, meaning not only do they feel emotions far more intensely, but they also have the energy resources to let them out in full force.

The ADHD brain struggles to distinguish between what are real, life-threatening concerns and what are minor problems. Thus, it doesn't matter how insignificant your child's issues are; it appears severe and overwhelming to them.

We cannot treat the emotional response of those with an ADHD diagnosis with a singular approach. Yes, medication may help, and so may all the other treatment options already mentioned, but if applied on their own, they will not deliver the outcome you seek, and you need to create and maintain a happy and stable environment in your home.

These are the unchangeable facts of ADHD and emotional regulation. Yet, knowing what you are up against doesn't mean you must remain a helpless onlooker to your child's emotional outbursts. No, knowledge empowers you, and as a parent of an ADHD child, every bit of power you can gain can become a treasured tool in your kit of skills for dealing with ADHD effectively. In this case, the treasured tool you seek is called emotional intelligence.

THE STEPS TO BECOMING MORE EMOTIONALLY INTELLIGENT

As mentioned, learning a new skill can be hard, but before you can persevere through that difficulty, you need to know what steps you must take. Again, it is like driving; you have to become familiar with the steps of the correct techniques before you can be any good at it. The process of becoming more emotionally intelligent consists of the following elements.

Acknowledging your emotions as something that makes a valuable contribution to your life is vital to your progress. Have you ever heard someone who stated that they don't tend to their emotions as they rely far more on their rational thinking? These people tend to think it is an excellent approach to life and managing their lives effectively. Maybe, they even said that logical thinking is much more reliable to turn to when needed. Is that someone, perhaps you, your mom, or dad? If so, it is time to reconsider your perspective, for research indicates that emotions play a vital role in rational thinking to the degree that those suffering from damage to the parts of their brain responsible for managing and understanding feelings struggle to make rational decisions (*6 Steps to improve your emotional intelligence*, 2018).

Start by asking people how they are feeling. Do so with a sincere interest in what they are experiencing at that moment. What is your go-to answer when you are asked how you are doing? I would guess, it is something like "I'm fine," or maybe just a simple "good" without any attempts to expand on your emotions.

How will your life change when you change your response? What if you don't just say "fine" or "good" but actually recognize and express your feelings? Can you do this without turning it into a lengthy complaint? For example, when you are feeling frustrated and exhausted, though it is only eight in the morning, your spouse asks you how you are feeling. Instead of saying "fine" or jumping onto the horse called Blaming and Justification, you express your feelings honestly. "I am tired and frustrated and have no idea how I will make it through this day or maybe even through the rest of the year. It leaves me feeling despondent that I put in all this effort to calm our child down; nothing seems to be an effective solution. But I know it will all look much better when I feel rested again. I just need a good night's rest." That would be an answer you can expect from someone who is emotionally intelligent. In these few sentences, you clearly identify your feelings and express them without blaming how you feel on someone or something else.

Emotional intelligence is about identifying and expressing your emotions and being more aware of what others are experiencing. When someone says they are sad or embarrassed, assure them it is fine to feel this way. Don't brush it off by telling them they'll feel better soon or get over it. Such an action would reinforce the current notion that emotions are not an acceptable topic to talk about, though they are.

You need to identify your emotions and see how you can use them to your benefit, and you need to accept the fact that you are feeling certain emotions and will do so for a while. Rather than wishing these emotions out of your life, accept that they are part of life and, at times, you'll experience feelings you don't like.

You can capture these emotions to record what you are feeling. You can choose to do so by writing in a journal. State why you are feeling this way and what the triggers were that stirred these emotions. By keeping a record of your feelings, it is easier to analyze why you are feeling a certain way. Writing your feelings down also creates some distance between your emotions and yourself, and it becomes easier to address them objectively.

The better you handle your emotions, the more effective you'll be in addressing the emotions your child is experiencing, even when they cannot express themselves effectively or accurately. Then, you can help your child to identify what they are feeling and how to communicate it effectively.

We can only teach what we know, so before you can teach your child—a child already starting with a challenged ability to express emotions—you need to understand your feelings. This is only possible by gaining greater emotional intelligence.

HELPING YOUR CHILD IDENTIFY AND EXPRESS EMOTIONS

What can you do to help your child overcome the challenges they are facing when their emotions are going through a peak?

Remain Calm

As a parent, you need to stay calm. Take a deep breath, and know that you are far better equipped to manage your emotions than your child is. Breathing deeply—in through your nose and out through your mouth—has a natural calming effect that will help you maintain your composure. Doing this several times will improve your stress levels drastically and allow you to control your emotions.

This is also an excellent time to shift your focus to what is positive. Know that during that moment, when your child is experiencing all these intense emotions, they can't move their focus from all that is wrong. They are completely immersed in the situation, but you can actively direct their focus away from what is negative to what is positive. By doing this yourself, too, you are modeling the behavior they can follow.

Ask how you can help them bring about immediate relief to what they are feeling, or you can even alert them to how they can help themselves to feel better and more effectively manage their emotions when they are feeling this way.

Teach Them to Reframe Their Thinking

Help your child to become aware of their thinking patterns and to gradually reframe them in a manner that is helpful and supportive of their needs. Reframing your thoughts demands that you take note of the things you are thinking and question whether they are accurate. Are these emotions and thoughts based on the reality of the situation, or are you misinterpreting them completely?

The next step is to help them to challenge and replace their unhelpful thoughts. Turn this exercise into a fun venture for you and your child. Just ask them what they are thinking about at that moment and listen attentively to what they have to say. Then, make suggestions of more emotionally intelligent thoughts to consider, and explore what it feels like to think these pleasant thoughts instead. You can even turn this into a game you play when your child's emotions get out of control.

Encourage Greater Connectivity With Their Feelings

A significant contributing factor to your child's inability to manage their emotions effectively can be attributed to their inability to identify what they are feeling. We all need to focus on what we are experiencing and then attach a name to the emotion to guide us in the proper, effective manner of expressing these emotions. ADHD children need to do this to an even greater extent. Initially, your child may not know the difference between anger, frustration, or disappointment. Their go-to emotion to express is merely anger. So, regardless of whether they are disappointed about not making the team or frustrated with a science project that won't work as they've planned, they may respond with anger.

An emotions chart can be a helpful aid in this regard. This chart shows images of characters expressing a range of emotions, and by looking at the chart, your child can quickly identify the image of how they are feeling instead of just acting out. By identifying your child's emotions, you can address their state more effectively. Remember, each time you are modeling this kind of behavior—going to the chart and identifying the emotion they feel and then addressing it correctly—you are setting an example of what they should do.

You can also up your approach a notch by asking them, during moments of greater calm, what emotions they are experiencing when they lose a game, struggle to find their shows, or can't seem to find answers they need in a school assignment.

Identifying Triggers

Triggers are those things that happen, are said, or your child may see, hear or even smell that can prompt an emotional response. The best approach to stop these triggers from having control over their lives is to identify them, as you can then define an appropriate response or even avoid them as much as possible without limiting your life. Triggers can sometimes manifest as your child being hungry. I mean, it is pretty normal to be more irritated, angry, or short-fused when you are hungry, hence the term "hangry." But what other triggers can cause your child's disruptive behavior? Work with them in identifying their triggers and, while doing so, teach them the needed skills to recognize them for themselves.

Once you have clarity on these triggers, decide what would be the best approach to handle these triggers. If it is hunger, make sure your child always has a snack nearby. This can improve their blood sugar levels and ease irritability. You can also decide what would be the best approach for them when they are confronted by their triggers. Compare this plan to the evacuation plan in an office building or apartment block. The trigger would be the fire alarm. If there is no evacuation plan, mass hysteria will break loose, and everyone will run for their lives, causing far more injuries and damage in the chaos than the possibility of fire perhaps. But if you have an evacuation plan in place, everyone knows what to do and how to react when the shrill alarm disturbs their peace. Now, they know where to exit the building and how it would be best to do so, and they minimize the casualties caused by hysteria because they are prepared for what may happen. Help your child to get a plan in place to minimize the casualties when their triggers disturb the peace.

Part of the evacuation plan includes that everyone has to meet at a specific spot deemed safe. Here, they know they can remain for as long as needed without being in danger. Identify a safe space for your child to turn to when their triggers send them on an evacuation routine. This will be a safe escape they can go to when the world becomes overwhelming.

Teach Your Child Techniques to Help Them Calm Down

When we face scary situations, they tend to be much worse if we don't know what is happening to us or what to expect. So, tell your child what is happening to them when they get stressed out. Your ADHD child is already alienated enough at times, and there is no need to leave them to wonder whether what they are going through is a normal response. Sometimes, just knowing what is happening to us is already calming us down a great deal.

What is happening to your child? They are experiencing a fight-or-flight response. This response kept our ancestors alive when they still had to face predators to find food—or on any other occasion when they left their caves. It is a biological response triggered by the release of stress hormones like cortisol and adrenaline, increasing heart rate and blood pressure, causing shallow but rapid breathing, and directing circulation away from the digestive system to ensure all resources are allocated to keeping the person alive. Therefore, when they become flushed, breathe rapidly, or feel their hearts pumping in their chest, they are only experiencing a natural response, as this is how they were designed.

The trick comes in understanding that while the response we are experiencing today remains the same as in the times of our ancestors, we have substituted the rainforest with the concrete jungle, and unless your life is in direct danger, the severity of this response is unnecessary. Once the threat was gone, the ancestors' stress hormone levels dropped, and they returned to a relaxed state. Today, the danger wasn't real, so it can't go away, and if you don't address being in a fight-or-flight state, it will persist.

The good news is that as your brain releases hormones that affect your body, you can use your body to reverse the effect and calm down your brain. Belly breathing is one such effective technique. As breathing becomes rapid and shallow when stressed, deliberately changing your breathing can calm the mind and body.

Belly Breathing

Belly breathing entails your child placing both hands on their belly area and then inhaling and exhaling deeply, focusing on how their belly expands to push their hands up and how it drops when they exhale.

Box Breathing

This helpful breathing technique brings the body out of the fight-or-flight state. It is very similar to belly breathing, but now your child will place one hand on their chest area and the other on the belly. As they take slow, deep breaths, they can focus on how the air moves their bodies and how they gradually begin to feel calmer and more relaxed.

Count to 10

I remember wondering as a child why people would always say to count to 10. I knew early on that 10 was not nearly far enough to calm me down. It was only much later in life that I realized it was not so much about the counting but that I had to shift my focus to something other than what I was upset about. So, yes, let them count to 10, 50, or 100—if they're super confident with math, or need an extra distraction, ask them to count backward from 100 in multiples of 7—just as long as they shift their focus to the counting and away from what upset them.

Other Soothing Techniques

Your child may find comfort in a specific object or action. It can be a blanket or soft toy they identify with to soothe their emotions. Identify any such aid and know where to find it when your child needs it the most.

Other soothing techniques include giving your child a hug to make them feel safe and accepted. Letting your little one know that it is okay to be in a sad or bad place at times can also help them to calm down.

Pets can be helpful too. Many people find calmness in stressful moments when they spend alone time with a family pet, soothing it and allowing the pet to distract their attention from all that is bothering them.

Soothing music can also be beneficial. Help your child to focus on the music and to listen to the tones and rhythm to help distract them from what is upsetting them.

THE BEST WAY TO TEACH IS BY MODELING DESIRED BEHAVIOR

Practicing what you preach is the best way to help your child overcome their challenges. Your child learns a lot from merely observing you. Without you even being aware of it, your child is watching your every move, and it is when you are under stress they learn how to handle their own stressors. I mean, it is a bit hypocritical anyway to tell your child to remain calm and to partake in activities to help them better deal with their emotions, but when push comes to shove, you behave in the exact manner you tell them not to.

So, take up an exercise regime to help clean your system of unhealthy stress and invite your child along. Include them in creative activities you do to distract your mind. These activities can take several forms, like dancing, playing an instrument, drawing or painting, scrapbooking, or any other activity you are interested in.

Talk about your emotions and show them that sharing how you are feeling is safe and acceptable. And, a big win, if possible, meditate together. Yes, this can be challenging, but your child may surprise you with enough practice.

IDENTIFY WHAT CAUSED THE FEELINGS

Disruptive emotions are primarily rooted in the lack of a basic need. When this is the case, the feelings you witness are only the symptom but not the cause of the problem, and you'll be much more effective in addressing the cause in which the emotions are rooted. Often, these causes are the need to feel safe and connected and to have healthy self-esteem. Then, there are also their needs to explore, experience love, and have a purpose, according to psychologist Abraham Maslow (Greco, 2020).

Talk to your child to determine why they are acting out. It may be anger that you are seeing, but the actual cause of their behavior might be their need to feel connected, triggered by rejection they faced during their day.

FOCUSING ON ANGER

Due to the challenges ADHD children experience in identifying their feelings, anger remains the most prominent emotion they express. Thus, we have to talk about anger. As ADHD makes all feelings more intense, it does the same with anger too. So, your angry child is really experiencing immense anger when they are expressing it in the most inappropriate ways.

As these emotions are so intense, they will likely apply any channel simply to relieve the pressure they are experiencing. Picture a volcano ready to explode. Once the pressure from deep inside the earth's core becomes so intense, there is no consideration of what the collateral damage will be when the hot lava is spewed into the air. Your child is the same. There are no bad intentions on their side, they just need to relieve the pressure they are feeling, and subsequently, there is collateral damage in the process.

You can guide your child more effectively by being mindful of the process and how it works. You can teach them that not every volcano explodes with similar destructive force. Sometimes, the impact is far less disruptive and hurtful to others just by holding back on the explosion.

It can also help them get away from what triggers the hot lava to build up and create a pressure point. Sometimes, the lava can also cool down when you exercise, get rid of all the pressurizing hormones, and replace them with cooling, feel-good hormones.

One more option will be to guide your child to use this energy for the greater good. If we can capture the heat energy radiated from an active volcano, we will have a lot of electricity to power the globe. That way, the negative or destructive force can become much more beneficial. So, instead of expressing their anger destructively, they use this energy for the greater good. Go and mow the lawn, or chop some wood for the fireplace. Maybe even go for a jog. It truly doesn't matter what it is, as long as your child can do it in a safe environment and use the steam they need to let go of positively.

What Makes Anger Worse?

Stress and anxiety are the worst factors increasing the challenges your child is already facing when they are angry. Exposure to stress and anxiety can multiply the intensity with which they are already experiencing anger. When this is the case, it can be easy to slip into a downward spiral where anxiety and stress cause increased anger, and the anger they are experiencing heightens the level of stress and anxiety they are experiencing.

Therefore, by helping your child to manage their stress, you will also positively impact the level of anger and anxiety they are experiencing. Be aware that some medications can increase the level of anger your child will experience. If this is the case with your child, adapting specific calming techniques will be even more beneficial to you and your family. Some of these techniques can ensure that your child remains protected by a set structure or routine of daily activities. Structure and routine offer children a safe environment as they have certainty of what is okay to do and what is not and what to expect throughout each day.

ASK FOR HELP

Mom, Dad, it would really help if you learned when to ask for help. How many parents try to push through on their own limited resources while support is available? Maybe, it is pride, or you think you will be a burden to others if you ask for help. It can even be that you don't want to come across as weak. These assumptions about asking for help are all wrong. People who ask for help when they need it come across as people who are confident enough in their ability to do what is expected of them that they know asking for help won't make them look weak. Being able to acknowledge any shortcomings and have the foresight to call in additional resources only shows your commitment to delivering the best possible outcome.

If you do not ask for help when you need it, how can you teach your child to reach out when they need help? Always live the advice and guidance you teach your child, as doing so remains a far more potent way of teaching than offering them hands-off, hypocritical instructions.

Wow, this was an immense amount of information, but emotional management is only one aspect of the comprehensive approach that can help you to address the challenges you and your child are facing. ADHD does come with a lot of baggage, and at some point, you need to learn the skills to let go of the unnecessary weight burdening your shoulders and pulling you down.

HEALING THE PAST AND THE FUTURE

About 6 million children in the US have been diagnosed with attention deficit hyperactivity disorder, or ADHD. Nearly two-thirds of those kids have another mental, emotional, or behavioral disorder as well. One of those conditions could be childhood traumatic stress.

— ANGELA NELSON

Another statistic we need to consider is that more than two out of every three children in America suffer some type of traumatic event that can have a lasting effect on them (Walsh, 2022).

When we look at the relationship between childhood trauma and ADHD, it reminds us of the age-old question: Which came first, the hen or the egg? Here too, both can be the answer you are looking for. It doesn't take long to realize that the relationship between ADHD and childhood trauma is highly intertwined and complex. One can cause the other and vice versa.

Furthermore, studies indicate that children with ADHD are far more likely to experience some childhood trauma, and both events affect similar brain regions (Nelson, 2022). The areas affected are the prefrontal and temporal cortex areas. Both are responsible for controlling decision-making, impulses, and emotions. This brings us back to what has been previously mentioned about ADHD and childhood trauma having very similar symptoms, and therefore, it is vital to contact a medical professional as soon as you notice any symptoms in your child so that you can address the matter most appropriately.

This leaves us to ask one crucial question: What constitutes childhood trauma? In simple terms, childhood trauma refers to any event(s) that can cause a minor to feel such a high level of fear that it gets locked into their mind, heart, and body. This fear response can stay with the child into adulthood if it stays unaddressed. The range of events that can cause childhood trauma is quite long. Here, you will find incidents of rape, being a victim—or witnessing a loved one be the victim—of any type of abuse, being in an accident, losing a loved one, going through a parental divorce, feeling rejected by an absent parent, or being a victim of bullying. While these events are some of the most familiar causes, they are not nearly all the causes of childhood trauma.

A 360-DEGREE APPROACH

Due to the nature of the relationship between childhood trauma and ADHD, addressing the symptoms of childhood trauma will bring improvement to the behaviors your child may experience caused by ADHD.

To address trauma effectively, you must take a comprehensive approach. As already discussed, this will demand that you take care of your child's mental and physical health. But this alone isn't enough. You would also have to include a greater diversity of steps in your approach. These steps would need to be aligned with the different stages of trauma recovery.

The Need for Safety and Stability

The first phase of trauma recovery demands that the survivor gets distance between themselves and the causes of their trauma. During this phase, it is vital to ensure your child is safe. It demands that you create a safe environment for your child or remove any threats from their current environment to stabilize it again. This stage demands that you protect your child and comfort them.

It is also important to note that after severe trauma, your child may take several weeks or even months to feel secure in any environment, even when they've experienced it as safe. It is, of course, a situation that is even worse when your child has been exposed to chronic abuse or if the traumatic event occurred in an environment where they used to feel safe.

The areas that need to be stabilized are not necessarily physical but can include specific parts of their being. For example, your child may have taken a step of boldness and put themselves out into a position beyond their comfort zone, like acting on a stage. Then, they were overwhelmed by severe stage fright when they had to perform, an emotion triggered by someone making a nasty comment regarding their acting abilities. This moment of humiliation may cause them such fear that the mere idea of doing something resembling the event—like presenting a verbal assignment or even acting on a romantic interest—may cause them to experience fear, holding them back. In such an event, their confidence would be the area where they need to feel secure and stable again.

The Need to Mourn

Traumatic experiences are always linked with a sense of loss. It can be that they may have lost a loved one or something less tangible, like their innocence or who they were before the event occurred. Let's revert to the stage fright incident. The child may have dreamt about themselves acting on a stage, being the main character in a play, but after the traumatic event, this dream is shattered. Giving up on a dream is definitely something that may cause your child to experience a sense of loss, and they have to mourn what they've lost.

Childhood trauma can present itself in many forms, and your ADHD child is more prone to have these experiences than a neurotypical child. I am not encouraging your child to remain safe and secluded at home instead of putting themselves out there. In fact, I am encouraging your child to do as much as they feel fit to do. Yet, in the same breath, I am encouraging you, as their loving parent, to be alert for any signs, to keep your ear to the ground, and to sometimes listen to the things *not* being said, to identify any cause of concern as quickly as possible so that you can help your child.

During the mourning phase, giving your child time to deal with the matter at their pace is essential. Be there to support and guide them, but don't rush them. Help them find suitable ways to mourn what they've lost and identify what they are feeling and why it has such a powerful impact on them.

The Need to Reconnect and Integrate Themselves Into Their World

After the mourning phase has passed, returning to the world you've escaped from is essential. You know that the key to success is not the number of times you've fallen down but how many times you've gotten up again. Your child needs to get up and be brave enough to approach life again. By encouraging your child to do so and providing them with the support they need to be able to, you are helping them move forward and enabling them to become stronger and more confident in their ability to overcome adversity.

This is when it is essential to emphasize that the events that took place aren't what defines their identity. How they approach the matter and overcome adversity testifies to who they are. They can rise much more substantially from the trauma they've experienced by becoming someone their peers can turn to for advice. This is the phase of trauma recovery that brings back hope in the mind of the trauma survivor, but it is impossible to reach this stage if you haven't experienced all the preceding stages of the process.

"Everyone has the right to have a present and future that are not completely dominated and dictated by the past" (*Phases of Trauma Recovery*, n.d., para 11). You can help your child free themselves from past events by teaching and modeling appropriate and effective trauma recovery techniques.

TECHNIQUES TO HELP EQUIP YOUR CHILD FOR TRAUMA RECOVERY

These techniques will equip your child to grow stronger after a traumatic event, and as this growth takes place, gradually, the symptoms will decrease, alleviating their symptoms and improving their quality of life. As you know, when their life gets better, so does yours, as you gradually restore a healthy equilibrium for every family member to flourish.

Your first response should be to let your child feel safe. While some kids feel safe when they are hugged or held, it may not be the best way to comfort your child. You know your child, and you know what makes them feel more secure; give them what they need so that their sense of fear and being lost doesn't last longer than necessary.

It is pretty normal to be upset when you become aware of your child's traumatic experience. I mean, for sure, when you learn about the trauma, it is normal to experience a surge of mixed emotions ranging from anger to feeling hurt. You, too, may experience a sense of loss and be highly concerned about your child, now and in the future. The traumatic experience can even trigger past memories of a trauma you experienced as a child. But these emotions are for you to handle, not to show to your child. It is best to at least try to subdue it, as your child may be looking to you for comfort and support, and if you are showing intense emotions, it can only leave them feeling their emotions more acutely. So, for what it is worth, try to remain as calm as possible to reassure your child that everything will be okay again.

When events cause chaos and unexpected change in your child's life, they can find an anchor in the stability of routines. Therefore, try to maintain the routine they are used to as much as possible. There is something strangely calming and soothing in the familiarity of a known routine.

Talking about the trauma and how it made your child feel is another way you can help your child gain a different perspective on what happened and process the events. While you may be eager to find out every detail of what occurred—and you are most likely to be ready to take revenge on the person who traumatized your child—it is vital that you don't push your child to share more than they are prepared to. Make time to talk to your child, and just allow them to talk about the event when they are ready, sharing their feelings as they are able to safely expose them to you.

These are some steps you can take at home to assist your child through this challenging time and to minimize the possibility of lasting effects limiting their life, now and as an adult. But there are also more formal aids to help your child overcome the challenges they are facing and improve their symptoms in the process.

It would help if you found a trusted professional to become your partner in the process of helping your child, as more complex therapies can only be administered by a trained professional. I am referring to cognitive behavioral therapy, also referred to as desensitization therapy, and other somatic modalities like TRE. Psychedelic therapy is another helpful aid in trauma recovery, but it isn't suitable for children.

ADHD, TRAUMA, AND SELF-ESTEEM

You most likely experienced some childhood event that devastated you, and it crushed your self-esteem back then. Similar events can also do grave damage to your child's self-esteem. Children spend a lot of their time surrounded by their peers, and children are way too harsh towards each other. I am not even referring to the dreaded school bully you might be convinced has an internal radar alerting them to every child with an existing inner vulnerability for them to pick on. Some kids just don't realize the impact of their words. "You are so slow," "No, I don't want David on my team. He never listens," "My brother says you are weird. That's why the teachers send you out of class to calm down." Often, your child may not even repeat the comments thrown at them during the day. As I said, not all negative comments are with ill intent. Sometimes, they are merely expressed out of ignorance. Nevertheless, let's not get bogged down on the reasons why your child is exposed to these comments, but rather how these comments can affect them and how you can support your child to overcome the obstacles keeping them from having healthy self-esteem.

Focus On Their Strengths

So much emphasis is placed on the negatives surrounding ADHD that we can easily overlook the benefits of the disorder. When last (if ever) have you sat down with your child and discussed the benefits of

ADHD, presenting it as personal strength to those like your child?

- **Hyperfocus:** As much as your child may struggle to focus on a single task, they also have the ability to hyperfocus. When your child takes on a task they enjoy, doing something they are interested in, they can remain focused. This ability can help them to excel in the areas they are interested in and outperform others who lack the ability to hyperfocus.
- **Resilience:** Most teachers consider ADHD children to be far more resilient than their neurotypical peers. Thinking about the challenges your child has already faced and overcome, it is evident that they are far more resilient—and have had plenty of practice in becoming more resilient—than their neurotypical friends. Yes, ADHD comes with many challenges, but it also forces your child to be stronger and better equipped to overcome setbacks.
- **Creative:** ADHD students often show the most creative genius in their classes. As your child has a different perspective on the world—caused by the fact that they have to approach everything in life differently than what they

would've if they weren't diagnosed with ADHD —they are naturally more creative.
- **Courage:** You know that your child's courage scares you at times. Yes, there are times when their courage can be downright irresponsible. Yet, in these moments, it is evident that your child won't stand back from what may scare many others.
- **Energy:** High energy levels are one of the aspects of ADHD that is extremely exhausting for parents. You are likely not tuned into the same high energy, and that is why it can be exceptionally tiring. But your child is energetic, always on the go, and depending on how you look at their behavior, it can reflect a vibrant life. Compared to many kids today who are lethargic and only want to sit behind screens, having high energy levels is a strength your child portrays.

Maybe, you feel that some of these benefits are a bit of a stretch. But then again, life often is what we make of it, and if you and your child are only going to focus on the challenges they are facing, then having ADHD can become an immense burden. Sometimes, when we dare to change our perspective on our circumstances, events, or life in general, an entirely new and different world reveals itself to us. So, seeking new perspectives by helping your child to see the benefits of their condition before being aware of their weaknesses and the accompanying challenges can boost their self-esteem tremendously.

Help Your Child Set Boundaries

Boundaries help us to protect what is important to us and keep us safe. Therefore, your ADHD child needs to set boundaries in their life too. The typical areas where boundaries are necessary are usually linked to their physical space for mental and emotional protection, time, and boundaries related to their body. The benefits they can reap from setting boundaries are that it enables them to be happier, as they feel more secure in the safe environment you've created with their boundaries. Healthy boundaries can improve your child's relationships and make them more productive. Yet, what is even more critical is that boundaries increase a sense of self-respect, and as it indicates that you respect yourself, others respect you too. It is also a way to boost your self-confidence as you care for your needs.

Therefore, helping your child identify what they need to protect with boundaries, what type of boundaries will be effective in doing so, and how they can benefit from this will improve their self-esteem and help them overcome this impact of trauma.

Placing Their Needs First

The foundation of self-care is to put your needs first. This means that you should guide your child to define their needs regarding safety and security, physical needs, or the need to feel loved and respected. If these are neglected, the chances of feeling depressed, anxious, stressed, or rejected are much higher. Therefore, teach your child that self-care is not a selfish act but something that can be incredibly beneficial to their state of being. It is only when their cup is full that they can make a contribution to the lives of others. This is, of course, a message that hits home very hard for some parents. You, too, may feel so consumed by the needs of those who depend on you that you neglect taking care of yourself. So, why not make self-care one of those lessons that you teach by modeling for your child, rather than telling them what to do and then doing the complete opposite yourself?

Guide Your Child to Pick a Supportive Circle

We become like the people we surround ourselves with. That is just one of life's undeniable truths. If your child is going to surround themselves with those who are negative the entire time, this will spill over to them too. The same is true when you surround yourself with positive friends who you can trust and who are helpful. Encourage your child to pick friends who are good to them, encourage them to become more confident, and be supportive when in need. This will help your child, and it will leave you feeling more relaxed too.

There are many ways the past can wear us down, and the only way to live a long and happy future is to let go of this baggage and pain. This is when your child will be empowered to live a life where they can progress. The foundation of effective social interaction is healthy self-esteem. Now that you have that covered, we can progress to explore helpful approaches to supporting your child in the world, beyond the safety of your home.

8

ADHD, SOCIALLY SPEAKING

ADHD is not a choice or bad parenting. Kids with ADHD work twice as hard as their peers every day but receive more negative feedback from the world.

— DRB

It's no secret that having a kid with ADHD is challenging. You have first-hand experience with the immense amount of stress and exhaustion the disorder causes in your life. I mean, you feel it. You know what I am talking about. You are painfully aware of how ADHD causes more challenges in your life, the life of your child, and that of their siblings, which all spill over again to the stress levels you experience. Even the simplest thing can be a struggle. Tasks like grocery shopping can turn into an exhausting experience as your child is overwhelmed by all the activities and items stimulating their brain. Taking a night off is another challenge, as the neighbor's kid no longer wants to babysit yours after that last incident nobody wants to talk about—at least not if it isn't behind your back, right? Those are things other parents take for granted.

While knowing exactly how hard parenting is for you, you remain aware that life is far harder for your child. Their ADHD demands so much more of them. Your child has to invest much more of themselves to enjoy a similar outcome to a neurotypical child, which is exhausting. Your child didn't choose this. They are born a certain way, but they are not alone. They have you, and together you can be a team, supporting and enabling each other to live a happy life.

THE SOCIAL STRUGGLES YOUR CHILD IS FACING

Your child is probably struggling to fit in socially. This challenge involves more than just them needing to work hard to make friends and be liked by others. Social inclusion forms a large part of their personal development, and they may be denied this inclusion from their circles as they are different.

Often, children with ADHD are considered by their peers to be naughty, rowdy, always getting into trouble, disruptive, and hard to befriend. This perception of children with ADHD is mainly caused by the vast confusion over their disorder. The signs of ADHD are often perceived to be part of the ADHD child's personality, making these concerns something they *"are"* rather than identifying them as the challenges they face. I recall an incident on the playground when I was about 13, and while sitting underneath a tree, completely mesmerized by the leaves blowing in the wind, I heard my name. A girl I only vaguely knew was walking towards me with another girl I'd never spoken to. The one who was a mere acquaintance just said, "hello," and walked on with her friend, and I remember feeling quite happy that she called me to say hi. But as they walked away, I overheard her friend asking her why she was so friendly with me as I was a "troublemaker." I remember how the beauty of that moment was crushed instantly, and for the rest of the day, I kept thinking of myself as a troublemaker. That other girl didn't know me at all, but she had the perception of me being a troublemaker, which stuck with us both.

The most common reasons for poor social interaction from an inattentive child are that they struggle to listen to others and, therefore, miss a lot of information shared. They are easily distracted midway through a conversation or game and may just walk away. When interactions become too loud or busy, they'll quickly feel overwhelmed and withdraw from the social circle they deeply want to belong to, seeking a place offering more security. Then, there is also the battle to understand social cues, and most miss out on what is said without being verbalized.

Social challenges brought on by hyperactivity are that your child comes across as rude due to their constant interrupting of others. This hyperactivity also causes them to talk a lot—and fast. Their ideas run wild, and they can struggle to focus on one subject. Yet, then, the complete opposite can also occur, causing them to become hyperfocused on a topic, draining and even confusing their social companions at times.

What are the challenges the impulsive child faces? They can be very goofy—which is, in a sense, still okay—but they have poor timing and don't know when enough is enough. You know that, at times, your child can come across as aggressive, and while there is no malintent involved, it can scare others who are not as familiar with them. Add to that their complete disregard for the personal space of others—and that they rarely have a perception of when is a good time to initiate a conversation and when to remain quiet—and suddenly your curious, creative child is being perceived as abrasive and rude.

Other children and their parents do not understand your child's obstacles, and they judge their behavior on the same scale as they would with a child without these challenges. Can you see how complex social interaction is for your child? Or, why can it so easily become an area in their lives that causes them to feel anxious?

SOCIAL ANXIETY AND ADHD

At the core of social anxiety is the overwhelming fear of being judged and scrutinized by others. Social acceptance plays a significant role during the different development stages your child is going through. Therefore, it is normal for the ADHD child to carry an even heavier burden when developing a fear of social situations, perhaps to the degree that they may prefer to avoid being social entirely. While this may be a matter of concern during childhood and adolescence, it is a challenge your child will also face during their adult years. Social anxiety impacts the lives of about 12% of all adults, and it does have a higher prevalence among adults with ADHD (Saline, 2022).

The symptoms of social anxiety are all rooted in a fear of not being accepted by others, and this fear can manifest in a range of ways. One common sign is not feeling comfortable talking to anyone beyond the safe barriers of family relations. These individuals also have a challenging time making new friends. Often, and understandably so, their behavior in this regard is just brushed off as them being shy. Nonetheless, these concerns have a much broader impact, as social anxiety also tends to create intense worry in your child. They may fear judgment, feel self-conscious, and be easily embarrassed. You need to understand that these fears are not merely fleeting moments that will pass soon. No, they can be so intense that they drag your child into full-blown panic attacks, causing them to perspire profusely and feel nauseous and shaky.

Social anxiety can be extremely limiting, and as developing social skills is such a necessary part of your child's development, it remains a vital concern.

HELPING YOUR CHILD OVERCOME SOCIAL ANXIETY

Developing the social skills to present yourself with confidence in social situations is a vital part of the development of every child. However, as your child is already struggling to overcome certain limitations regarding emotional management and their ability to read social cues, it is even more vital for them to become social-skill smart. If they don't, the number of challenges they'll have to overcome now and during their adult years will only become more overwhelming.

Social anxiety can lead your child to struggle to make friends, get along with peers, be part of a team, or collaborate on a mutually desired outcome. Their lack of understanding of the proper way to address others and to behave in social settings can cause them to hurt the feelings of others unintentionally and to be hurt in return. These are often contributing factors to the ADHD child's aversion towards school. School, truly, is where your child will be challenged on many levels. If it is not in the classroom, where their behavior may be frowned upon, then it is their lack of focus when completing assignments. These two factors may not be uncommon in the school set-up, as many other neurotypicals often struggle with them too, but break time often makes the day okay for these kids. For those children, school can be more than a place where they have to learn and adhere to instructions; it is also where they meet their friends, have social bonds with peers, and can have fun. For your kid, the opposite is true, as even break times can be challenging and lonely times when they are further misunderstood.

If no efforts are made to address this concern, it is a challenge that will drag on from one year to the next, never improving, continuously evolving, and getting worse. But how can you assist?

Tips to Address Social Anxiety

Now, let's just first take a moment to acknowledge that even for the parent of a neurotypical child, it would be stepping onto very thin ice to step in and assist them with their social challenges. Far too often, it happens that parents step into situations—with only the best intentions—but cause much more significant damage. It can happen so quickly that your child is labeled as "the one whose mommy or daddy needs to step in." The *worst* you can do is to directly address the kid who is making your child's life at school exceptionally difficult. The optics of doing this need to be treated sensitively, and you can place yourself and your child in a tricky situation where the abused is perceived as the abuser. It will be much easier for the parents of your child's bully to present you as an abusive parent who stepped out of line addressing their child directly than for you to prove how their child treats your child at school.

Thus, opt for a different approach. Let's discuss some tips that will help your child and not cause any more challenges to overcome.

Don't Address an Abuser

Before you do anything, make it evident to your child that you are on the same team and that you'll allow them to lead and take you in a particular direction; you'll be their wingman (or wingwoman). This means you are now playing on your child's territory and trusting their judgment. So, if they don't want you to talk to Mary's mother about her daughter constantly making snarky remarks toward them, then don't. Don't even say a thing when you run into her at the supermarket. Doing this will break the bond's trust, and you need to be in an alliance with your child if you genuinely want to help them deal effectively with this challenge.

Practice the skills they'll need on the playground and in the wider world, at home. As your child may not have many friends, they don't have the many opportunities other kids may have to hone their social skills. Therefore, employ your immediate and extended family members to become part of the efforts you and your child are putting into adopting and mastering the social skills they need. Use a family board game to practice sportsmanship, or have some family over for a barbeque in the backyard to enable them to play with the kids in the family, following the rules and maintaining appropriate behavior. When failure or a social faux pas occurs, don't address the situation in front of onlookers but rather have a chat aside with your child, guiding them on what they did that wasn't acceptable, how to fix the situation, and what they must do to improve on their behavior.

Arrange Playdates

You can also arrange playdates with kids you are comfortable with that are compatible with your child. A playdate may initially be daunting for your child, but having this take place in a familiar environment where they feel secure can help. You'll, of course, also be around—though not hovering over your child—within hearing distance to guide the situation from afar. Having these playdates run successfully can boost your child's confidence to continue what works well at home in a less secure environment too.

Consider Social Skills Training

You can fulfill this role for your child or reach out to someone they trust to serve as their mentor. If you choose the latter, you may find that your child is more willing to cooperate when they've identified the person they want to fulfill the role. Remember, once you have this kind of buy-in from your child, your chances of success immediately increase. Keep in mind nobody is getting along with everyone, but it will benefit your child a lot if they can get along with most, and this is only possible if your kid is comfortable and equipped to present themselves in a socially accepted manner.

Being a Mentor

What does being the social mentor for your child entail? Feedback, feedback, and more feedback. Not only do you have to give immediate feedback on how they've erred, but you need to do so in a non-judgmental and supportive manner. I feel your pain as the realization that you must be even more diligent in staying on top of your emotional management. But, I am not done yet. You'll also have to give feedback focusing more on the positive actions taken during these situations. So, you'll need to make a greater effort to applaud the few things they've done right while only pinpointing the things they've done wrong in a non-judgmental way, even when you are deeply upset about what they've done.

Can I just remind you at this point about how critical taking care of yourself is? If you don't take time out for self-care and to recharge your batteries, the quest of being a supportive parent to your ADHD child can quickly become so overwhelming you may be defeated before you've made any innings at all.

Focus on One Area

The next tip is to avoid confusion by focusing on only one area of concern during every social interaction opportunity. Before the social visit you've scheduled as a chance to hone their skills, you should identify what areas they need to work on. Pick one area, and sit your child down for a team talk to help them understand why their specific behavior is a concern, what is best not to do or say, and what options they have to choose from to make their behavior socially acceptable. Then, after the playdate, party, or even school day, sit down and discuss what was good about it and what your child feels they need to improve on. Help them understand what may have been a more effective approach in a similar situation or why someone is angry at them over something they've said.

The best way to teach remains to practice. You can't expect your child to do what you tell them to do during social situations when you don't even do that yourself. By modeling the behavior you expect of your child, you give an example of what excellent social skills look like, how it is beneficial to have these skills, and what it looks like in action.

Family—both immediate and extended, depending on your situation—can play a vital role here, too, to help your child practice their skills. Home can even be a place where roleplaying can occur to lay the foundation of what your child should do and how to respond to a range of possible scenarios.

Get Professional Help

You can call on a professional in this regard too. If your efforts are not bearing any fruit, you may need to book a few sessions for your child with a social skills therapist. In the care of a professionally trained expert, your child may be keener to adopt the needed skills. However, calling on such a service would still mean that you collaborate with the professional to practice the skills at home and provide the expert with feedback on what went well or which areas are still in desperate need of improvement.

Improve Their Peer Status

Call on the school to help you with improving the peer status of your child. What does this even mean? Peer status refers to what other children your age think of your child. Your child may have a peer status even with kids they don't know, as this status is based on their reputation, which evolves from how peers observe their behavior and how others treat your child. For example —even when your child does have a reasonable number of friends—if, during classroom time, the teacher portrays an underlying irritation, annoyance, or frustration toward your child, this behavior is witnessed by every child in the class, contributing to the perception of your child. Younger kids, especially, are prone to take the same approach their teacher may have towards your child. Once peer status has been created, it is tough to change or shed it unless you move towns, perhaps, and start on an entirely new page somewhere else. (Note, this is not a preferred solution as the change your child will go through can be so disruptive the situation will quickly be the same in the new setting.) Rather, aim to address the neurotypical adult in the specific relationship. When a teacher approaches a child with love, care, and patience, this approach will widely be adopted by your child's peers too. So, ask your child's school to collaborate in this regard.

As a parent of an ADHD child, you are persistently bombarded with more significant challenges than any other parent. Most parents find being a parent to a teenager the most challenging part of their parental journey. The teenage years are known for severe emotional fluctuations as hormones kick in and often take over your child's personality. It is no different for your child, and you, too, will—or might already—be facing the brunt of being a mom or dad to a teenager.

How do you deal with the added strain in your home, and how can you make it through these stormy years, still progressing and supporting your child's journey toward adulthood?

THE ADHD TEEN

They said I could pass at normal, that I was clever and no one would ever know. They lied. Not about passing. The lie was hidden beneath, in the desire for me to be the same as them. I am extraordinary. They should have helped me soar, be more, not less.

— ANNA WHATELEY

School is a place where cliques can rule the lives of every living being on the premises. They are the ones who determine who is "in" and who fails to meet the requirements they've set for social acceptance. As a teenager, it is normal to want to be included in these cliques, as that serves as testimony that you are okay. Their acceptance, or even the lack of their visible rejection of your existence, is similar to a stamp of approval.

Whether you despised these cliques with every fiber in your body or were the leader of the pack when you were a teenager, it often comes as an unexpected surprise to run into the same social hierarchy when you meet the other kids' parents at your child's school. It can happen when you are chaperoning at the school dance or busy at the bake sale. There are always parents who see an opportunity to show off their children's accomplishments. While there is nothing wrong with taking pride in your offspring's exceptionalities, it is much more fun being the one flaunting the phone with a million impressive pictures in the gallery than to be witnessing the fame parade from the sidelines. Just once, you want to be the one who can trot from table to table to let them know your child is exceptional too. Regardless of age, escaping social acceptance remains a challenge.

Now, your ADHD child is not oblivious to your heart's desires, but simultaneously, they are also painfully aware that living up to expectations will most likely not happen for them. Yet, this only explores the social pressure they feel via your involvement in their life at school, and we haven't even touched on the direct pressure they are exposed to at school.

CHALLENGING SOCIAL SITUATIONS

The pressure is on your child as they move into their teenage years. Why? Because as children progress into their teens, they naturally become more independent, self-motivated, and passionate about their purpose as they prepare for adulthood. Your child's brain is falling three years behind the brain of the average neurotypical teenager. Thus, while your child may physically appear to be on the same level, they are not, and the faster teenagers progress in life, the more obvious the distance between your child and the others becomes. This distance stands out like a sore thumb in the high-pressure environment of junior high and, especially, high school.

Now, we can move on to the raging hormones and natural moodiness typical of teenagers, to which ADHD is no aversion. It is no wonder some parents feel that the ADHD symptoms they've learned to understand and thought their child could manage are suddenly beyond what they can comprehend. Maybe, you are left convinced that your child's symptoms got worse amidst your dreams of seeing some improvement.

Grasping all of the above can be challenging. Acknowledge that this may be a more profound obstacle than expected, as this will help to free you from the burdening desire for social acceptance.

Problems at School

The problems your teen may face at school exceed a mere desire for social approval. There are also possible failed romances, broken hearts, and a persistent increase in what academics demand of them. Throughout all these challenges, you'll need to aim to remain the person they can turn to who can offer guidance.

I vividly remember how I lost my heart to the most attractive boy in my class (or at least, he was to me). I was about 13, and we had just recently relocated to Italy. There was no doubt in anyone's mind that I was the odd one standing out from the rest, and at that age, an age when fitting in is vital, it was a tall order to expect any kid in my class to want to be associated with me, and yet, it was when I fell in love for the very first time. I was utterly smitten, as one tends to get at that age. For the first time, going to school wasn't as bad as I had something to look forward to during the day— staring at the back of his head. I know how crazy that sounds now, but when you are that age, it doesn't matter if you found what you believe is love.

After some time passed, and he still didn't notice me, I realized it was time for me to step up my game. I planned to share my feelings with him in my broken Italian, and the ideal time would've been during the lunch break. However, my courage disappeared as I was heading in his direction, and I decided to instead capture my feelings on paper. This turned out to be another social failure. I wanted to pass him the letter during class, but as I tried to get his attention with the letter in my hand, the teacher saw me and told me to hand over the note. I cringed in embarrassment but was extremely angry at the same time. I thought, what gave her the right to ruin my life like this? I ensured she could see how angry I was for the remainder of the class.

She called me to her desk when the period was over and told me two things. The first was to never make such bold statements as I did without having some certainty that the other person sees me in a similar way. The second: to use the correct spelling and words to pin down my next love declaration.

After the event, it took me a while to warm up to her again. But now, I often think of this teacher and how much it meant that she was looking out for me, protecting me, and offering me guidance from that moment onward. When parents or any other adult step into such a caring role for a teenager, they may never receive any appreciation for their contribution until many years later. Yet, this delayed appreciation doesn't rob the moment of its value.

Another tricky social situation where your child can benefit from your guidance is when they enter a state of conflict at school. Social circles during the teenage years can be a place of immense rivalry, and they are bound to endure some friction or conflict during this time. You can use roleplay to teach them to turn around and walk away from conflict or how to end the situation if they are placed in a position that leaves them feeling uncomfortable.

Then, there is, of course, the academic side that becomes much harder as they grow older. This is kind of a double-whammy concern as their workload increases in volume and intensity. So, while your teenager has to commit themselves to focus on far more complex work and lengthier assignments, they would also have far less time to be active, explore, and walk around. Because they have delayed development in certain aspects of their being, the academic side of teenage years can be a challenge, not only for them but for you too.

HOW TO HELP YOUR CHILD NAVIGATE LIFE THROUGH TEENAGE YEARS

There are several ways you can offer your teenager the support they need to navigate life and get through their turbulent teenage years without lasting injury. Most of these tips don't require much except for you to be an understanding adult who treats your teenager with similar respect as you would treat an adult friend.

Roleplay

Roleplay can be a handy tool to practice acceptable or desired social interaction. Some generic scenarios you can prepare your child for are how to approach people, what is considered a proper way to express a romantic interest, or how to behave in specific challenging social settings. It would've helped me if my teacher would have opted for roleplay to guide me on how to address the love interest I had rather than trying to pull the plug on my efforts. But, in her defense, I didn't trust her or anyone else with that information before I went over to action. This brings me back to why it is important to cherish and expand the trust between yourself and your child. If mutual trust wasn't a characteristic of your relationship prior to their teenage years, it could be hard to set it as the norm now. However, it is never too late to build this trust.

Expand on Trust

When your relationship with your teenager is built on trust, it will be much easier to support them socially, as you'll be let into their social circles, and you can guide them along with the friends they keep.

The same trust will also cause them to attach greater value to the example you model regarding social interaction. Never underestimate how much influence you can have by setting an example of the type of behavior you want to see in them.

Share Interests

You are strengthening your bond by sharing your interests with your teenager and asking them about theirs. It is how you improve the relationship and encourage them to trust you with their secrets. It remains the most effective way to monitor their activities without causing any hostility. I've had parents telling me how they would regularly scan their teenager's phones and how tricky it can be to get hold of these devices and be able to log into them. While it may be an effective manner to keep tabs on your teenager in the short run, it is not a method I would recommend. How would you feel about someone else invading *your* privacy by snooping on *your* phone? Even if there is nothing to hide, it remains a gross disregard for privacy and boundaries. By disregarding their personal boundaries, you void everything you might have taught them about boundaries in the past.

Show Empathy

A better approach to gaining inside information about what is happening in their lives is to show authentic empathy. Listen to what they have to say, but also take note of the things they don't say, for a lot is often communicated without ever saying a word. Through this approach, you create a space where your teenager knows they can go without being judged or exposed to criticism. Instead, share some of your past mistakes or tell your teenager about what you wished you did differently when you were their age. As parents are so painfully aware of their mistakes and flaws, they often miss that their children don't see these things. I've found that children, and especially teenagers, can be reluctant to share sensitive information about something they've done with their parents as they perceive their parents as these flawless people who have never done anything wrong and, therefore, won't understand what they are going through. Be sure to shed this image as people, in general, are much more open to sharing their secrets with others when they know they are merely human too.

Expand Their Circles

Another approach is encouraging greater involvement and expanding their social circle by joining clubs and taking up more extracurricular activities. Here, they can befriend others within a safe and controlled environment. While these kids may not become their best friends, it will help to have more people in the school passages they are familiar with at school.

Academic Support

While you may have been able to help them with assignments during their younger years, not all parents are equipped to assist with high school math or science. These subjects were challenging for me during school, and most of what I've learned is now long forgotten. Asking me to offer support with either of these subjects —and probably several other subjects, too—would be a futile quest, as I don't think I'd be able to make any valuable contributions. Therefore, it will most likely be beneficial to your child, you, and your relationship to instead hire the necessary academic support to give your child the help they need.

It is also helpful to gain the cooperation of your child's school. You can ask that extra time be allowed for your child to finish their tests, exams, and assignments. While you would always want to encourage your teenager to exert themselves to reach their full potential, the damage it does to their self-esteem to always try to achieve goals that are just out of reach for them is just not worth it.

Planners and schedules may have been something you've helped your child with during their younger years, and now you expect them to take care of these themselves. That is perfectly fine, but when you hand them the responsibility to take care of these organizational responsibilities, don't leave them abruptly without them understanding what it would entail to stay on track. Rather than leaving them on their own, maintain a distance requiring your involvement to a lesser degree.

HANDLING EMOTIONAL DYSREGULATION

While we all deal with fluctuating emotions daily, the increase in hormones teenagers experience makes these fluctuations more severe. Add to that your ADHD teenager's existing challenges to manage their feelings, and you can sit with a volatile situation on your hands.

Additional causes contributing to fluctuations in your teen would include a lack of social acceptance from their peers. Other reasons for concern would be when they are more prone to show external symptoms like defiant behavior while internalizing their stress, anxiety, and depression.

It is widely accepted that when your teenager reaches adulthood, they should've mastered specific skills to be sufficiently equipped to face adult life's obstacles. These skills include their ability to identify their feelings as well as the feelings of others, how to pursue their goals without feeling anxious, and knowing how to soothe overwhelming emotions.

A lack of skills needed for emotional regulation presents itself as self-harm, acting out, aggression, avoidance, or even abuse. Furthermore, teenagers struggling with emotional dysregulation tend to abuse alcohol or other substances (Stade, 2017).

You can support your teenager to enhance these skills, empowering them to have greater emotional regulation, by modeling the effective use of coping mechanisms. An additional approach is to encourage them to adopt several skills to improve how they manage their stress more effectively.

Sustaining healthy habits like getting enough sleep, exercising, and maintaining their body's needs through a healthy and balanced diet will also be beneficial. Furthermore, by keeping routines familiar, you'll give your child a stable anchor which can ground them during these turbulent times.

TIPS FOR TEENS

Creating a home environment where your teenager gradually takes on more responsibility and feels secure can significantly benefit them in handling the challenges they face at school—both socially and academically—with greater ease.

One of the most frustrating things, as someone with ADHD, is that it feels like others constantly make decisions on your behalf. This is also disempowering since you never get to stand on the other side of decision-making, so you never understand the purpose of these decisions, what they are supposed to achieve, and why taking responsibility in this manner is vital. Allowing your teenager to have an input or an opinion when family routines are set or rules established can serve as an effective approach to introduce them to more responsibility and to understand why it is vital to adhere to these rules.

Encourage positive feedback as the norm in your home. Constantly seeking the positive side of any event—not only regarding your ADHD teenager but every family member—serves as the foundation of an environment where your teenager can feel accepted. This acceptance can and will make life in this challenging developmental stage much more bearable. It equates to knowing that even if they are rejected in all the social circles at school, there is still a place where they are accepted just for who they are.

One of life's undeniable principles is that actions have consequences. Work with your child to identify challenging behavior that they need to address. Then, let them determine the consequences they must face if they overstep the boundaries they've set to address the problematic behavior. For example, if your child agrees that they are sometimes overstepping the boundaries of others by interrupting conversations whenever they feel the need to say something or that their go-to response is anger that is now getting out of hand, then they'll have to go without their phone or any other device for a week. You can determine the behavior and the consequences, allowing your child to have a say.

Lastly, I can't overemphasize how important a set routine is during emotionally turbulent times. Even today, I am still very attached to my routines, and they bring me comfort through their familiarity in many ways. My routine is a form of self-soothing behavior. Giving your child, regardless of age, this security can make your life easier and deliver exceptional results, requiring minimal effort.

These are some of the challenges you'll face during your child's teenage years. However, you and I both know that these challenges are merely the tip of the iceberg. So, let's discover some more tips that will help to ease overcoming these obstacles and that have proven to be effective, not only in my life but also in the lives of many others with ADHD, stepping up to living life at full capacity.

EVERYDAY COPING TOOLS

> *If you can't fly then run, if you can't run then walk, if you can't walk then crawl, but whatever you do you have to keep moving forward.*
>
> — MARTIN LUTHER KING

FOCUS

The need to encourage greater focus and a longer attention span is always a pressing matter in the life of someone with ADHD. While a neurotypical person may experience some off days when they struggle to focus—if they've had a poor night of sleep, for instance—an individual with ADHD is constantly working to maintain their focus.

By default, there is nothing you can do to change this, but you can help your child set measures in place to aid in this quest. We've already covered several steps that will contribute to your child's ability to focus, like eating healthy food, getting enough sleep, and being active—preferably outdoors. These are the basics you need to instill in them. The next step is to encourage them to take similar initiatives independently. At some point, you want them to *want* to eat healthy, knowing it will benefit them, and no longer because they are forced to do so.

Practicing mindfulness is another step that has brought about many benefits for me. Mindfulness training is a proven method to improve focus in children and adults with ADHD, and it helps to improve the symptoms of depression and anxiety (*Helping children with ADHD focus without medication: 7 tips for parents*, 2021). Nevertheless, your child can also practice becoming more mindful by following a few simple steps. For example, taking a quiet moment to breathe deeply can increase their focus throughout an exam, test, or to get an assignment done.

You can also try to use brain training or behavioral therapy. In the end, you'll only know what works best for your child by trying several options and, from there, determining what is bringing you the best results.

TRANSITIONS

For most small kids, transitions can be tough. This is evident in the typical toddler behavior of crying when parents are ready to depart from a playdate. However, gradually, as we grow older, it becomes easier to shift from one task to another, to leave one place and move on to another. This gradual shift doesn't happen for a person with ADHD. Throughout life, this remains a challenge. I was devastated and felt extremely lost when my parents moved to Italy and, then, only a few years later, moved back home. I couldn't find my way, and I felt overwhelmed. The immense changes to my environment, routine, and entire world were daunting, and I felt depressed, lonely, and like nobody understood how I was feeling. This was a major transition that I had to struggle through with very little understanding from others, as it was before I was diagnosed. But just as disruptive as this move was to me, change can be hell for your ADHD child—moving house, schools, or simply leaving the house to go to school. Things that appear to be simple to others—like switching from working on one subject to another, from watching a show to taking a bath, or from stopping to play to having supper—can cause feelings of irritation, being more scattered than usual, or even experiencing excessive fatigue.

This is caused by the lack of executive functioning to control our behavior when we need to shift between tasks or settings.

You can help your child by giving them advance notice, maybe even twice if necessary. For example, if you know that you need to leave a certain place in 10 minutes, tell your child that you are going in 10 minutes and, again, 5 minutes before the departure time. That may not completely resolve the resistance you may get, but it will surely reduce and make it easier for your child.

Other helpful adjustments to ease the process include keeping the number of individual steps needed to complete a task to a minimum, giving instructions slowly and deliberately, going the extra mile, sticking to familiar routines as much as possible, and breaking down large and overwhelming tasks into smaller bits. As your child grows older, always encourage them to apply the same steps to their approach when they work independently. It is how you can prepare your child for independent living.

One more thing that can distract them from the coming transition is offering a reward or emphasizing the positive outcome you are working towards. A few years ago, a mother shared with me how she used the latter technique to overcome several challenges at home. Her son of 10 loved horses and would do anything to go horse riding. She used this as his reward to get him to do his homework and complete several other chores. Together, they worked out a point system. If he finished his homework on time, he would get five points, and making his bed and getting ready for school would be another five points. On a Friday afternoon, they would tally the points, and every point would count for one minute he could spend at a farm nearby riding horses. "Yes," she said, "it does mean that some Saturdays I spend a couple of hours at the farm, but at least my weeks ran much smoother; Benji felt that he contributed to his success, and it was a great form of exercise in the fresh air. It is a system that works for us." I think that is the key to success—experiment until you find a system that works for you.

ADHD RUSH

As already mentioned, not all kids with ADHD are hyperactive, but when your child is, it can be very exhausting to maintain their pace in life. They are also fidgety, which can be disruptive in a class set-up, and while they are easily bored, no distraction entertains them long enough. Many parents have suffered the embarrassment of getting their kids off of statues, benches, or even shelves in the local grocery store, as they will climb without thinking.

You can help your child to slow down. When you do, pick your words wisely. It is my understanding that our brains—all human brains, not only the ADHD brain—are wired to place less focus on negative statements. For example, when you say to your child, "Don't run," the brain only registers "run." Then, that is naturally what your child will have the urge to do. However, the ADHD brain also experiences pathological demand avoidance and will shut down in the face of demands like, "Walk," "Slow down," or "Sit here." Instead, when instructing them, try a positive question such as, "How about slowing down?" or "Can you sit here for me?" These are both clear instructions that will help to convey what you expect of them while also allowing them a sense of autonomy.

Another way to reduce this active behavior is to give them something to focus on. While the world went crazy over fidget spinners a couple of years ago, nobody realized what a nifty little aid these could be to help your ADHD child to focus. Before that, we had squeeze balls that would help to improve our focus. Even before I knew I had ADHD, I would often study with a ball in my hand, as it made me feel at ease, as if I was calmer deep inside, which helped me to focus a little longer too.

MEALS

Food is often a cause for conflict in a home with an ADHD eater—or non-eater—as many parents feel the pressure of having a child whose appetite is suppressed by the medicine they need to take, and getting any healthy food into an already malnourished body is a challenge. Rely on your inherent creativity when you prepare meals. Offering healthy food presented in a fun manner can do wonders for kids. One idea that comes to mind is to cut sandwiches in different shapes or use a cookie press to create a special snack. You can also add color to meals.

Some parents have specific table toys with which the child can play as long as they eat. This serves both as a reward and a distraction. Another option is to get your child interested in the meal by getting their help in the kitchen before you set the table. The more you grow comfortable with applying different approaches to address one challenge, the more you'll realize that most action steps bring about a range of benefits. It is a two-flies-with-one-swat situation, the kind of approach that benefits any overwhelmed and tired parent. For example, having your child help you prepare supper gets them interested in the meal and also serves as a time to reduce your workload, while they get to feel important and that they are contributing.

It is also good practice to have them play outside before having a meal as this way, they'll get rid of all their energy and sit down at the table hungry and ready to eat. Eating at the same spot or sitting in the same chair at the table also increases familiarity, benefiting your child.

LOSING THINGS

Several parents make it a habit to go through the lost and found box at school weekly. They often find things their children don't even realize they've lost. It is how it is, and you can make your life easier by marking every valuable item your child has. This makes it easier to prove ownership when you find it and to quickly identify the things that belong to your home.

A great habit to model is to always place certain things in specific spots. Hanging the house keys on the hook and leaving the remote in the coffee table basket are just some examples here. You can also mark certain items with bright tape to make them easier to find when misplaced. No system is perfect, however, so it's best to have a backup plan. I'm still guilty and will only realize that I don't know where my house keys are when I leave my house. This has caused me to run late several times, so I decided to attach a soft bright pink toy to my keys. Though I still try to always place them back on the key hook where they belong, finding my keys—when I haven't put them away—has been much easier since I added the toy.

Part of being a parent to an ADHD child is accepting that there are things you'll be able to work on and improve but also that certain things will never change. Losing and misplacing possessions is one of the latter. Your child can't help it. They may try to avoid these situations, but when it occurs, accept that it is part of who they are. If you are going to lash out at them, you are merely increasing the stress and anxiety levels you'll have to address later and not positively impacting the situation. Apply your humor, as humor always lifts the mood. One parent in a support group I've attended started a small side business creating clothing stamps that would state, "Sorry, I was lost again. Please return me to (name)." For me, this lady was an inspiration and the personification of knowing what she needed to accept, changing what she could, and knowing the difference.

ACCIDENTS

Rooftops, tall trees and walls, busy streets, fireplaces, and the list of risks for injury on your property can grow infinitely. You can try your best to keep your child off the rooftops and repeatedly warn them about the risk of injury, yet the chances remain that they may get injured.

Be prepared for this by having a stocked first-aid kit in the home, as you never know what injury you might need to treat until you can get your child to the emergency room.

Like any first-time parents who invest a lot of thought and effort into baby-proofing their home, you too need to safety-proof certain areas of your property. When you do, try to think like them; be fearless in your imagination to accurately identify all possible risks your child may face. Investing time into developing their motor skills is also good, as the chances of injury decrease when their balance improves.

There is another type of accident that may also surface at times. Part of the ADHD prognosis is poor executive function and interoception—the ability to perceive one's own internal bodily state. This means that your child's brain may not alert them to a full bladder in time. Depending on your child's age, it goes without saying that such an incident can be very humiliating and won't do their confidence or social acceptance any good. Try to remind your child regularly to go, or if you know that they'll be out, set their watch to remind them to go regularly. By going to the bathroom often enough, you can take over bladder control and drastically reduce the risk of these accidents.

HOMEWORK BATTLES

Homework or any other academic-related assignment will always remain a challenge. Some helpful tips in this regard would be to have a reward system. I prefer reward systems above facing the consequences for the lack of action, as this works well with dopamine-hungry ADHD minds. Yes, as discussed earlier, it is essential to establish that every action has a reaction, but when it comes to encouraging your child to do something they don't like to do, focus on the positive.

Lately, there are more no-homework schools than before, and placing your child in such a school will remove much stress from your life. You can also employ specific practical solutions like having your child sit on an exercise ball or even letting them work from a desk where they can stand up. Standing remains a better position for extended focus. Also, like with any other child, keep their work environment distraction-free. Remove any unnecessary wall decorations or clutter that only serve to distract attention.

CHOOSING THE RIGHT SCHOOL

Today, parents have a vastly greater range of options regarding schools than only a few years ago. Apart from no-homework schools, there are also schools focused on more practical lessons where your child would be less constrained to their desks.

In schools with smaller classes, teachers are less overworked and have more time to give every child individual attention and understand their unique needs. It may be a pricier schooling option, but your child will benefit in many ways, making this investment money spend well.

The Montessori schooling method is a proven technique that has produced many of the world's brightest minds. It is also a method that is very accommodating to the learner with alternative academic needs, and as the Montesorri grading system is different from the conventional school system, it can help your child mitigate the three-year delay they have compared to their peers.

Encourage your child to move around physically at appropriate times during the day, as this will also ease the desire to move or fidget when they are expected to remain seated quietly. Lastly, I encourage all parents with ADHD kids to research adaptive schools. The system in these schools is designed in such a manner to consider your child's unique needs, and the curriculum is based on the child's abilities, learning style, and behavior.

TEACHERS

The teachers at your child's school are vital contributors to your support network. Therefore, even if you choose a conventional school, seek out a school with a reputation for understanding the needs of ADHD children and employing teachers who know and understand their unique needs and have experience dealing with them. Attend any school meetings where systems are put in place to accommodate children with different schooling requirements and rely on the staff to support your child's academic success.

CONCLUSION

Why fit in when you were born to stand out?

— DR. SEUSS

For the longest time, my deepest desire was to fit into the environment I was placed by forces higher than myself. I often struggled to understand why I was here, why I was different, and even more importantly, why nobody understood me the way I was, not even my parents. I was convinced that I was the problem, the failure, and even that I was flawed beyond measure. It is difficult to explain, challenge, or express, especially when you don't have the vocabulary to do so effectively. Also, to your knowledge, no other way of being exists—you only know a world wrapped in the symptoms of ADHD, as that is what you were born into.

I wanted to change myself. I wanted to be someone else, someone who fitted into my home, my family, my school, my life, my everything. I would drive to stress and anxiety. I would often feel depressed because that is what happens when you are creating a version of yourself merely to survive—a shield, to help you present yourself as the person you think others want you to be, someone who gets through life with fewer obstacles to overcome. It is an impossible quest, like trying to fit a square peg into a round hole. It just doesn't work unless something gives in. If your child is the peg and the hole is the world, I can promise you now that it won't be the hole that will give under all the pressure applied to make something fit that just doesn't.

As a parent of ADHD children, it is crucial to accept your situation and make the most of it. Once you shift your perspective away from all the things that are wrong or challenging to what is good—and the fact that you have a very interesting, although a bit unorthodox, child capable of achieving extraordinary things on their terms—life becomes much easier.

Changing my behavior and the way I think was difficult. I realized that everything started with me and that if I didn't change something, I would always be angry with myself and life. Facts are consequences of the way we think. I started to focus on thinking kindly about myself and others, empathizing with them. I have to say that by understanding myself, I realized that others around me have their problems and may also need help in their turn.

I learned to think carefully about what I do and how I do it and to want to do something the right way. I let the positive results stimulate me. I started to appreciate my successes, even the smallest ones. I put fertilizer on the earth, and I created the perfect context to be able to be proud of myself. Having already reached maturity, changing the subconscious was—and still is—training, an exercise in which you have to skip all negative influences. When you have ADHD, you don't have time for thoughts that drag you down.

I learned to organize my head. Everything that does not help me grow, be good to myself, or stay positive, I skip. I apply everything I wrote in this book, and I feel good knowing I have some tools I can use.

As an adult, you already have the key life experience and understanding of what it means to have balance. With patience, you can teach your child how to reach this level too. Always ask them how they feel. If they're sad, be their support, but also show them that they can change their condition on their own. Show them that we can control our emotions and are in charge.

Show your child the importance of good values in life. Encourage them to like being dignified, respect themselves, and be fair. Show them how good it is to have a calmer mind, and what an uplifting feeling it is when you respect the needs of your mind and body. You, as a parent, try to teach them so that they have as few disappointments, and as many beautiful moments and memories, as possible.

> *The way we talk to our children becomes their inner voice.*
>
> — PEGGY O'MARA

For the child or teenager with ADHD, I want to say it doesn't necessarily get much easier, but you will get better at managing your life. ADHD requires a holistic approach to address the various concerns you may be dealing with, and initially, this may sound like a lot of work, but it is also a blessing. As there are so many techniques you can employ to relieve the impact of what you are experiencing, you can try a multitude of options to identify the practices and habits that best suit your unique needs. Never wish to change yourself or to hide your inner flame, but always work towards improving the brightness of the flame you are radiating. Explore every aspect of your being, and as you become more familiar with your identity, you'll be able to identify your unique strengths and determine how to leverage them in your favor. Never look back on past mistakes for reasons other than to seek life lessons and admire how far you've come. Then, give yourself a pat on the shoulder for being an amazing and unique person.

Dear parent, I know you are going through tough times, moments when you may feel overwhelmed and overshadowed by all you are facing, but there is hope. By reading every chapter of this book, you've familiarized yourself more and more with the obstacles ahead, and from greater awareness stems better preparation leading to outstanding success. Throughout, I've tried to show you your child's point of view, which is very real for me, as it is my perspective on the world too. But I've also covered the science behind what you are facing, as understanding the biology behind ADHD makes it easier to accept the symptoms. The same is true for the challenges you and your child may face regarding managing emotions, overcoming past frustrations, social challenges, academics, and surviving but also thriving during the volatile teenage years.

For far too long, the world has perceived ADHD as a disability. My wish is that you stay committed to observing the positives rather than being obsessed with the negatives of ADHD and that you remain focused on the opportunities instead of the limitations.

If you've enjoyed this book and felt it spoke to your heart and mind, please pay forward some kindness by leaving a positive review.

REFERENCES

The ADHD and ODD link in children. (2020, October 9). ADDitude. https://www.additudemag.com/oppositional-defiant-disorder/

ADHD and when misbehaving becomes more than "playing up." (n.d.). Aspriscs. https://www.aspriscs.co.uk/news-blogs/adhd-and-when-misbehaving-becomes-more-than-playing-up/

ADHD success stories. (n.d.-b). Understood. https://www.understood.org/articles/en/adhd-success-stories

Alder, S. L. (n.d.) *"Never give up on someone with a mental illness. When 'I' is replaced by 'we', illness becomes wellness." ~Shannon L. Alder.* Sanvello. https://www.sanvello.com/community/quotes/post/6922232

Anderson, S., Colon, I., & Prelle, L. (2019, December 19). *Are society's new expectations of teens too much?* The Live Wire. https://thelibertylivewire.com/2655/features/are-societys-new-expectations-of-teens-too-much/

APA Dictionary of Psychology. (n.d.). American Psychological Association. Dictionary.apa.org. https://dictionary.apa.org/mental-disorder

Arthur Conan Doyle Quotes. (n.d.). BrainyQuote. https://www.brainyquote.com/quotes/arthur_conan_doyle_134512?src=t_truth

Barkley, R. (2022, October 28). *What is executive function? 7 Deficits tied to ADHD.* ADDitude. https://www.additudemag.com/7-executive-function-deficits-linked-to-adhd/

Breaux, R. (2020, August). *Emotion regulation in teens with ADHD.* CHADD. https://chadd.org/adhd-news/adhd-news-caregivers/emotion-regulation-in-teens-with-adhd/

Brodey, D. (2022, April 19). *Adult ADHD: What it really feels like.* Psycom. https://www.psycom.net/adhd/adult-adhd-what-it-feels-like-to-have-it

Brown, N. M. (2022, November 7). Childhood trauma and ADHD: A complete overview & clinical guidance. *ADDitude.* https://www.additudemag.com/adhd-and-trauma-overview-signs-symptoms/

Brown, T. E. (2022, September 20). *7 Truths about ADHD and intense emotions.* ADDitude. https://www.additudemag.com/adhd-emotional-regulation-video/

Cassidy-Brown, A. (2022, March 9). *Study shows link between gut bacteria and ADHD.* Henryford. https://www.henryford.com/blog/2022/05/adhd-gut-microbiome-link

Castle, J. (2019, March 6). *ADHD and Appetite: Tips for kids.* The Nourished Child. https://thenourishedchild.com/child-adhd-no-appetite/

Causes of ADHD: What we know today. (2019, September 27). American Academy of Pediatrics. HealthyChildren. https://www.healthychildren.org/English/health-issues/conditions/adhd/Pages/Causes-of-ADHD.aspx

Causes - Attention deficit hyperactivity disorder (ADHD). (2021a, December 24). NHS. https://www.nhs.uk/conditions/attention-deficit-hyperactivity-disorder-adhd/causes/

"Cherish The Children Marching To The Beat Of Their Own Music. They Play The Most Beautiful Heart Songs" Vinyl Decal 27" X 10" : Tools & Home Improvement. (n.d.). Amazon.com. https://www.amazon.com/Cherish-Children-Marching-Music-Beautiful/dp/B00KWH8CN8

Coleman Tucker, G. (2014, November 3). *Channing Tatum on his ADHD and dyslexia.* Understood. https://www.understood.org/en/articles/channing-tatum-on-his-adhd-and-dyslexia

Cronkleton, E. (2021, August 12). *What are the differences between and ADHD brain and a neurotypical brain.* Medicalnewstoday. https://www.medicalnewstoday.com/articles/adhd-brain-vs-normal-brain#:~:text=Research%20shows%20that%20in%20people

Culture Vs. biology: What causes ADHD? (2022, March 31). ADDitude; ADDitude. https://www.additudemag.com/what-causes-adhd-symptoms/

Dahl, D. (2022, August 7). *ADHD quotes about the neurodivergent way of paying attention*. Everyday Power. https://everydaypower.com/adhd-quotes/

Data and statistics about ADHD. (2022, August 9). Centers for Disease Control and Prevention. https://www.cdc.gov/ncbddd/adhd/data.html

Davidson, K. (2020, February 5). *Mood food: 9 foods that can really boost your spirits*. Healthline. https://www.healthline.com/nutrition/mood-food

Definition of dysgraphia. (n.d.). Merriam-Webster. https://www.merriam-webster.com/dictionary/dysgraphia

Diagnosis of ADHD in adults. (n.d.). CHADD. https://chadd.org/for-adults/diagnosis-of-adhd-in-adults/

Dopamine. (2022, March 23). Cleveland Clinic. https://my.clevelandclinic.org/health/articles/22581-dopamine

Dickson, T. M. (2022, February 21). *"Why do I get so angry with the ones I love most?"* ADDitude. https://www.additudemag.com/adhd-how-to-control-your-emotions/

Discover exactly what ADHD feels like everyday. (n.d.). ADHD Collective. https://adhdcollective.com/what-does-it-feel-like-to-have-adhd/

Dix, M., & Klein, E. (2022, June 1). *What's an Unhealthy Gut? How Gut Health Affects You*. Healthline; Healthline Media. https://www.healthline.com/health/gut-health

Dodson, W. (2022, November 17). *How ADHD ignites rejection sensitive dysphoria*. ADDitude. https://www.additudemag.com/rejection-sensitive-dysphoria-and-adhd/

Doyle, A., & Sherrell, Z. (2022, June 22). *The 11 best ADHD apps for 2022*. Healthline. https://www.healthline.com/health/adhd/top-iphone-android-apps

Dyslexia. (n.d.). Merriam-Webster. https://www.merriam-webster.com/dictionary/dyslexia

Ellis, R. R. (2022, October 3). *What's the best exercise to manage ADHD symptoms?* WebMD; WebMD. https://www.webmd.com/add-adhd/exercise-manage-adhd-symptoms

Gill, T., & Hosker, T. (2021, February 10). *How ADHD may be impacting your child's social skills and what you can do to help.* Foothillsacademy. https://www.foothillsacademy.org/community/articles/adhd-social-skills

Greco, F. (2020, October 19). *What are your emotional core needs?* Www.yourpsychologist.net.au. https://www.yourpsychologist.net.au/what-are-your-emotional-core-needs

Hasan, S. (2022a, May). *ADHD.* Kidshealth. https://kidshealth.org/en/parents/adhd.html

Hasan, S. (2022b, May). *Parenting a child with ADHD.* Kidshealth.org. https://kidshealth.org/en/parents/parenting-kid-adhd.html

Helping children cope after a traumatic event. (2022, September 9). Child Mind Institute. https://childmind.org/guide/helping-children-cope-after-a-traumatic-event/#block_bbede789-dc0c-46b6-9489-6be91bfca5f6

Helping children with ADHD focus without medication: 7 tips for parents. (2021, May 3). RTOR. https://www.rtor.org/2021/05/03/helping-children-with-adhd-focus-without-medication-tips-for-parents/

Hoffman, J. (2013, September 10). *What does ADHD really feel like?* Today's Parent. https://www.todaysparent.com/kids/kids-health/what-does-adhd-feel-like/

Holland, K. (2021, October 28). *The history of ADHD: A timeline.* Healthline. https://www.healthline.com/health/adhd/history

How to develop a measurable and effective ADHD treatment plan. (2017, April 27). Navigating ADHD Inc. https://www.navigatingadhd.com/uncategorized/develop-measurable-effective-adhd-treatment-plan/

It's okay to put yourself first sometimes: Developing self-care. (n.d.). CHADD. https://chadd.org/adhd-weekly/its-okay-to-put-yourself-first-sometimes-developing-self-care/

Jean-Philippe, M. (2021, January 26). *55 of the most powerful Martin Luther King Jr. quotes.* Oprah Daily. https://www.oprahdaily.com/life/relationships-love/g25936251/martin-luther-king-jr-quotes/#:~:text=%22If%20you%20can

Keeping calm under pressure. (2017, November 14). Psychological Health Care. https://www.psychologicalhealthcare.com.au/blog/keep-calm-pressure/

Kinman, T. (2016, March 22). *Gender differences in ADHD symptoms.* Healthline; Healthline Media. https://www.healthline.com/health/adhd/adhd-symptoms-in-girls-and-boys

Laguaite, M. (2022, August 25). *Symptoms of ADHD in girls.* WebMD. https://www.webmd.com/add-adhd/childhood-adhd/adhd-symptoms-girls

Louw, K. (2021, February 28). *How to improve social skills in children with ADHD.* Verywell Mind. https://www.verywellmind.com/how-to-improve-social-skills-in-children-with-adhd-20727

Low, K. (2022, April 22). *What it's like for kids with ADD.* Verywell Mind. https://www.verywellmind.com/understanding-children-with-adhd-20686

Maguire, C. (2022, October 28). *Build back your child's social skills in 7 steps.* ADDitude. https://www.additudemag.com/how-to-improve-social-skills-adhd-children/

Managing attention deficit hyperactivity disorder (ADHD) in teenagers. (2021, July 5). Raising Children. https://raisingchildren.net.au/teens/development/adhd/managing-adhd-12-18-years

Mansfield, B. (2021, August 26). *The way we talk to our children becomes their inner voice. Your Modern Family. https://www.yourmodernfamily.com/way-talk-children-becomes-inner-voice/*

Max's story - Managing ADHD through diet. (n.d.). Nutritional Weight and Wellness. https://www.weightandwellness.com/resources/client-success-stories/maxs-story-managing-adhd-through-diet/

Mental Illness is nothing to be ashamed ofbut stigma and bias shame us all.-Bill Clinton. (n.d.). Easterseals New Jersey Blog. https://www.eastersealsnj.org/blog/its-time-to-stop-the-stigma-surrounding-mental-illness/mental-illness-is-nothing-to-be-ashamed-ofbut-stigma-and-bias-shame-us-all-bill-clinton/#:~:text=New%20Jersey%20Blog-

Mikami, A. Y. (2021, April). *Friendship problems? How parents can help.* CHADD. https://chadd.org/adhd-news/adhd-news-caregivers/friendship-problems-how-parents-can-help/

Mindfulness can help you manage ADHD at any age. (2021, July 22). CHADD. https://chadd.org/adhd-weekly/mindfulness-can-help-you-manage-adhd-at-any-age/

Myers, R. (n.d.). *Effective consequences for ADHD kids.* Empowering Parents. https://www.empoweringparents.com/article/effective-consequences-for-adhd-kids/

Nelson, A. (2022, September 29). *Trauma, kids, and ADHD: Is there a link?* WebMD. https://www.webmd.com/add-adhd/childhood-adhd/adhd-traumatic-childhood-stress

Newmark, S. (2022, November 18). *10 Supplements and vitamins for ADHD symptom control.* ADDitude. https://www.additudemag.com/vitamins-minerals-adhd-treatment-plan/

Other concerns and conditions with ADHD. (2022, August 9). Centers for Disease Control and Prevention. https://www.cdc.gov/ncbddd/adhd/conditions.html

Phases of trauma recovery. (n.d.). Trauma Recovery. https://trauma-recovery.ca/recovery/phases-of-trauma-recovery/

Porter, E. (2018, September 17). *Parenting tips for ADHD: Do's and don'ts.* Healthline; Healthline Media. https://www.healthline.com/health/adhd/parenting-tips#what-to-do

Price, K. (n.d.). *Feelings chart for calming corner - with printable.* Himama. https://www.himama.com/learning/child-activities/activity/feelings-chart-for-calming-corner

A quote by L. Todd Rose. (n.d.). Goodreads. https://www.goodreads.com/quotes/6956976-behavior-isn-t-something-someone-has-rather-it-emerges-from-the

Raising low self-esteem. (2020, February 6). NHS. https://www.nhs.uk/mental-health/self-help/tips-and-support/raise-low-self-esteem/

Rejection Sensitive Dysphoria (RSD). (2022, August 30). Cleveland Medical Professionals. *Cleveland Clinic.* https://my.clevelandclinic.org/health/diseases/24099-rejection-sensitive-dysphoria-rsd#:~:text=Rejection%20sensitive%20dysphoria%20(RSD)%20is

Richardson, M. (n.d.). *Nature: How connecting with nature benefits our mental health*. Mentalhealth. https://www.mentalhealth.org.uk/our-work/research/nature-how-connecting-nature-benefits-our-mental-health

Rodden, J. (2022, November 18). *What is executive dysfunction? Sign and symptoms of EFD*. ADDitude. https://www.additudemag.com/what-is-executive-function-disorder/

Russo, A., & ADHD Editorial Board. (2022, November 16). *ADD vs. ADHD symptoms: 3 Types of attention deficit disorder*. ADDitude; ADDitude. https://www.additudemag.com/add-adhd-symptoms-difference/

Saline, S. (2022, March 30). *Where does "Introvert" end and social anxiety begin?* ADDitude. https://www.additudemag.com/introvert-social-anxiety-adhd-adults/

Schreier, J. (2020, February 24). *Helping a child with ADHD develop social skills*. Mayo Clinic Health System. https://www.mayoclinichealthsystem.org/hometown-health/speaking-of-health/helping-a-child-with-adhd-develop-social-skills

7 Ways to reframe your thoughts towards growth. (n.d.). My Easy Therapy. https://myeasytherapy.com/2021/06/29/7-ways-to-reframe-your-thoughts-towards-growth/

17 Things to love about ADHD!. (2022, June 24). ADDitude; ADDitude. https://www.additudemag.com/slideshows/benefits-of-adhd-to-love/

Sherrell, Z. (2021, July 20). *What are the benefits of ADHD?* Medicalnewstoday. https://www.medicalnewstoday.com/articles/adhd-benefits#strengths-and-benefits

Silny, J. (2022, June 22). *What my worst days with ADHD feel like*. ADDitude. https://www.additudemag.com/slideshows/what-does-adhd-feel-like/

Sinfield, J. (n.d.). *How to create healthy boundaries with ADHD*. Untapped Brilliance. https://untappedbrilliance.com/how-to-create-healthy-boundaries-when-you-have-adhd

6 Steps to improve your emotional intelligence [YouTube Video]. (2018). TedX Talks. In *YouTube*. https://www.youtube.com/watch?v=D6_J7FfgWVc

Skogli, E. W., Teicher, M. H., Andersen, P. N., Hovik, K. T., & Øie, M. (2013). ADHD in girls and boys – gender differences in co-existing symptoms and executive function measures. *BMC Psychiatry, 13*(1). https://doi.org/10.1186/1471-244x-13-298

Social development. (n.d.). Office of Population Affairs. https://opa.hhs.gov/adolescent-health/adolescent-development-explained/social-development

Spina Horan, K. (2021, December 31). *7 Ways ADHD can be seen in the brain*. Psychologytoday. https://www.psychologytoday.com/za/blog/the-reality-gen-z/202112/7-ways-adhd-can-be-seen-in-the-brain

Stade, L. (2017, February 5). *The 10 emotional skills every teen needs to be taught*. Linda Stade Education. https://lindastade.com/the-emotional-skills-every-teen-needs-to-be-taught/

Stanborough, R. J. (2020, December 15). *Dehydration and anxiety: Understanding the connection*. Healthline. https://www.healthline.com/health/anxiety/dehydration-and-anxiety#hydration-and-anxiety

Story, C. M. (2022, June 30). *The 6 best herbs for ADHD symptoms*. Healthline. https://www.healthline.com/health/adhd/herbal-remedies#Combinations-may-work-better

Symptoms and diagnosis of ADHD. (2022, August 9). Centers for Disease Control and Prevention. https://www.cdc.gov/ncbddd/adhd/diagnosis.html

Symptoms of Inattentive ADHD. (2019, May 22). Hillcenter. https://www.hillcenter.org/symptoms-of-inattentive-adhd/

Tartakovsky, M. (2021, March 14). *ADHD & kids: 9 tips to soothe tantrums*. Psych Central. https://psychcentral.com/childhood-adhd/adhd-kids-9-tips-to-tame-tantrums#9-tips

Taylor-Klaus, E. (2022, February 17). *Are My Child's Worsening symptoms due to puberty? Or a chemical imbalance?* Additudemag. https://www.additudemag.com/does-adhd-get-worse-with-puberty-teen/

Treatment - Attention deficit hyperactivity disorder (ADHD). (2021b, December 24). NHS. https://www.nhs.uk/conditions/attention-deficit-hyperactivity-disorder-adhd/treatment/

20 Things parents wish people knew about ADHD. (n.d.-a). Understood. https://www.understood.org/en/articles/our-community-weighs-in-20-things-parents-wish-people-knew-about-adhd

Walsh, L. (2022, September 27). *Understanding child trauma*. Samhsa. https://www.samhsa.gov/child-trauma/understanding-child-trauma

Watson, S. (2021, March 9). *ADHD Hyperactive-Impulsive Type*. WebMD. https://www.webmd.com/add-adhd/childhood-adhd/adhd-hyperactive-impulsive-type

What is box breathing? (2021, April 8). WebMD. https://www.webmd.com/balance/what-is-box-breathing

Your day is getting better - starting now. (2022, April 15). ADDitude. https://www.additudemag.com/slideshows/adhd-famous-quotes-for-a-bad-day/

Zietsman, G. (2020, August 7). *A naughty, mean child might be hiding a psychological condition*. Health24. https://www.news24.com/health24/Parenting/Child/Mind/a-naughty-mean-child-might-be-hiding-a-psychological-condition-20200807-5

Made in the USA
Las Vegas, NV
26 February 2023